PRESERVING PARADISE

PRESERVING PARADISE

Why Regulation Won't Work

DAVID L. CALLIES

UNIVERSITY OF HAWAII PRESS / *Honolulu*

Printed in the United States of America
99 98 97 96 95 94   5 4 3 2 1

Library of Congress Cataloging-in-Publication Data

Callies, D. L. (David L.), 1943–
    Preserving paradise : why regulation won't work / David L.
Callies.
        p. cm.
    Includes bibliographical references and index.
    ISBN 0–8248–1576–9
    1. Land use—Law and legislation—Hawaii.   2. Land use—Law and
legislation—United States.   I. Title.
KFH458.C34   1994
346.96904'5—dc20
[349.690645]   93–28244

University of Hawaii Press books are printed on acid-free paper and meet the guidelines
for permanence and durability of the Council on Library Resources

Contents

To my wife and partner, Dr. Jane Ryburn Starn, who has taken on a larger role in the raising of our blended family than we had fairly anticipated, and to our children and stepchildren, Sarah, Melinda, Andrew, and Sean.

Acknowledgments

My sincere thanks to the Estate of James Campbell, Kamehameha Schools/Bernice Pauahi Bishop Estate, Land Use Research Foundation of Hawaii, and State of Hawaii Office of State Planning for helping to fund the research and writing of this book; to Carlito Caliboso, Robert Ferrigno, Karla Winter, Mike Medeiros, Linda Dragas, and Wayne Costa, present and past students of the William S. Richardson School of Law, for research assistance; to Jan Yamada, my secretary (whom I share with three patient colleagues), for typing draft after draft; and to Dan Davidson, Os Stender, Carol Rose, Baird Kidwell, Sheldon Zane, Clint Churchill, Roger Evans, Ed Henry, Aaron Levine, David Ramsour, Barry Cullingworth, and Kem Lowry, who reviewed drafts of all or some of the chapters. Finally, I would like to acknowledge the seminar paper and directed research paper of law students Madelyn Purcell and Terry Kondo, whose efforts helped shape some of the thoughts in this book.

Abbreviations

BACT	best available control technology
BLNR or Land Board	Board of Land and Natural Resources
CDUA	Conservation District Conditional Use Application
CFR	Code of Federal Regulations
CZC	Comprehensive Zoning Code
DGP	Department of General Planning
DLNR	Department of Land and Natural Resources
DLU	Department of Land Utilization
DOH	Department of Health
DP	development plan
EIS	Environmental Impact Statement
EPA	Environmental Protection Agency
FAR	Floor Area Ratio
FCZMA	Federal Coastal Zone Management Act
FEDC	Foundation and Empire Development Corporation
FIRM	Flood Insurance Rate Map
FWS	Fish and Wildlife Service
HAR	*Hawaii Administrative Rules*
HCDA	Hawaii Community Development Authority
HCZMA	Hawaii Coastal Zone Management Act
HEIS	Hawaii Environmental Impact Statement
HEPA	Hawaii Environmental Policy Act
HFDC	Housing Finance Development Corporation
HHA	Hawaii Housing Authority

HRC	Honolulu Revised Charter
HRS	*Hawaii Revised Statutes*
LUO	Land Use Ordinance
NEPA	National Environmental Policy Act
NMFS	National Marine Fisheries Service
NPDES	National Pollution Discharge Elimination System
OSP	Office of State Planning
POTW	publicly owned wastewater treatment works
PSD	prevent of significant deterioration
RCH	Revised Charter Honolulu
SIP	State Implementation Plan
SMA	special management area
SMP	shoreline management permit
TDR	transfer of development rights
USCA	U.S. Code, Annotated
USSCT	U.S. Supreme Court
YWCA	Young Women's Christian Association

PRESERVING PARADISE

CHAPTER 1

Regulatory Takings

A Hypothetical Case

On January 1, 1990, Foundation and Empire Development Corporation (hereafter FEDC) purchased 200 acres of land on Oahu's Leeward coast for the purpose of developing a resort-recreational community. FEDC is an international landholding and development conglomerate incorporated in California with worldwide revenues of about $800 million on assets valued at about $4 billion. Previously owned by Kamaaina Pineapple and Sugar, Inc., the land is part and parcel of a large plantation that due to market conditions has fallen on hard times and needs the cash to stay financially afloat. The land is mostly flat, with about 1,000 yards of ocean frontage, about half prime agricultural land (*mauka*, or toward the mountains; inland) and half marginal agricultural land (*makai*, or toward the ocean). Half of the prime agricultural land is classified by the State of Hawaii as conservation. The remainder of the 200 acres is classified as agricultural under the state land-use law. In addition, the 1,000 yards of ocean frontage land is classified as an area of particular concern due to sweeping views and public recreation potential under the state's coastal zone management statute. The remains of a *heiau* are discernible a short way from the beach, as are stones representing an old trail leading from the remains along the shore and up toward the mountains. The development plans for the City and County of Honolulu classify the *makai* portion as the "regulatory" coastal zone, as well as preservation with a preservation zoning classification from the county Land Use Ordinance (LUO), and classify the *mauka* portion as agricultural with an agricultural zoning classification from the same LUO. FEDC purchased the property in order to develop an eighteen-hole golf course and associated resort hotel on the *makai* portion of the property, with single-family residences on one-third-acre lots on the remaining *makai* and *mauka* portions. To do so FEDC must obtain a variety of permissions and reclassifications from the state and the county, including county shoreline management permits (SMPs) and reclassification under both state and county land-use laws. FEDC has also been advised by the Corps of Engineers that due to the parcel's proximity to a wetland and the ocean FEDC will need a dredge and fill permit. After four years, FEDC has been successful in none of its endeavors, having received no final answers from either the state or local government. In addition, the County of Honolulu is seeking a $30 million "impact fee" for the golf course, plus approximately $15,000 per dwelling unit and $10,000 per hotel room in traffic, solid and liquid waste disposal, and water impact fees. Moreover, the state and the county are seeking to have 50 percent of the houses set aside for low-income residents. The county is also seeking funding for all or part of a medivac helicopter with ocean rescue capabilities. Frustrated beyond endurance, FEDC files suit in federal and state courts alleging a taking of property without compensation and without due process of law, which is contrary to the Fifth and Fourteenth Amendments to the U.S. Constitution.

What does this mean?

Why did this happen?

What will happen next?

Before turning to a brief summarization of the answers to these questions—which are intertwined with the main themes of this book—several things are worth carefully noting from this hypothetical case.

1. Most of the property has been used for agricultural purposes—an open space use that most of us would value "good"—for many years. The rest of the property is in various "preservation" categories that many—except perhaps the property owner and other owners similarly situated—would consider good, or appropriate.

2. The proposed use will take much of the property out of an open space use and convert it to a "built" environment,

which many would consider either "bad" or "less good" than before.

3. The proposed use will take the rest of the property and convert it into an alternative open space use, certainly no less open and no less (perhaps even a little more) accessible than before, and which demonstrably uses no more water and chemicals than before, but which many would nevertheless consider "bad" or "less good."

4. The previous uses are either all or partially no longer economic. If the landowner can't do something else with the property, the developer can't use it at all under its present zone classification, except for part of the proposed golf course.

5. Conditions required by government for development are all for laudable public purposes, but only some of these conditions are necessary because of the proposed development; the rest are virtually unrelated to problems that the development is expected to either cause or exacerbate.

6. The developer is not "local" and has no other property in Hawaii, nor does it have any plans to acquire any. It is therefore irrelevant to the developer what government and the community may think of it for litigating to defend what it sees as its property rights, nor is it concerned about later governmental retaliation against its other interests or projects.

7. It has cost the developer hundreds of thousands of dollars in interest and other carrying costs while applying for the various permits and reclassifications needed to proceed with the project.

8. As appears below, Hawaii has one of the most sophisticated and plan-oriented (albeit time-consuming) land-use regulation and development-permission systems in the United States, if not the world.

9. Hawaii is a land of decidedly limited area and breathtaking but fragile natural beauty and resources.

10. The state and the counties have the authority to regulate the use of land for the health, safety, and welfare of its people.

11. Private property rights are guaranteed by the Bill of Rights in the U.S. Constitution; thus, their "taking," even for a public purpose, requires compensation.

Regulatory Takings and Private Property

The tension between land use and land regulation has bedeviled land policy for centuries.[1] However, the notion that the U.S. Constitution protects private property from government overregulation through zoning, development conditions, subdivision codes, and the like is barely seventy-five years old. In 1922, Justice Oliver Wendell Holmes of the U.S. Supreme Court held that if a regulation went "too far" it could be a taking of property protected by the Constitution. Justice Holmes also noted that government could hardly go on if every time a general law diminished the value of property, government had to pay for it, and that property could be regulated to a certain extent. The question is, to what extent? Just what is "too far" and what happens when government reaches that limit?

What the U.S. Constitution says is helpful, but not determinative. The main clauses are the Fifth and Fourteenth Amendments. The Fifth Amendment provides that private property shall not be taken except for a public use and upon payment of just compensation. Its principal purpose was to protect private property from physical acquisition by government for mainly private purposes (that is, redistribution among private citizens) and without payment or compensation to the landowner. Government always has the power to take, or "condemn," private property, but for governmental purposes only, and the government must pay for it. The Fourteenth Amendment requires that property shall not be taken without due process of law. It says nothing about compensation or, for that matter, about public use. Its primary purpose is to assure that when property is taken by government, it is done so only after fair hearings, open and prompt.

Landowners have used both amendments with increasing frequency to charge government with taking property through strict land-use controls. Federal and state courts have applied a variety of standards in attempting to decide when such regulations do in fact "take" property. Some things are clear:

1. There is such a thing as a "regulatory" taking under both the Fifth and Fourteenth Amendments. Neither applies to so-called "physical" takings alone.

2. When a taking occurs, compensation is an available remedy. Simply voiding the offending regulation is not sufficient.
3. Regulating property so as to totally devalue it is a regulatory taking requiring compensation unless any use of the property would be dangerous. Thus, for example, designating a large lot as "park" on a city zoning map and refusing any private use whatsoever would be a regulatory taking, unless the lot were on the slopes of a steep and unstable precipice.

Some things are not clear:

1. How much use must be left to the landowner under a land-use regulation? Existing use? Economic use? Investment-backed expectations?
2. Does it make a difference what the public purpose of the regulation is? To prevent nuisance? To protect health and safety? To protect welfare?
3. How many of an owner's property rights need to be taken and how does one divide them? If all mineral rights are regulated away, leaving surface and air rights intact, is that a regulatory taking? If 10 acres—out of 100 acres that are otherwise economically developable—are designated "park," as suggested above, is that a regulatory taking?
4. What conditions can government place on the "right" or "privilege" of developing private property?

The U.S. Supreme Court has attempted to answer these questions twice in five years, each time in a trilogy of cases, first in 1987 and again in 1992. The 1987 trilogy[2] attempted to answer three questions:

1. When is a regulation a taking? Depending upon how closely one reads the opinion, the answer is either whenever all economic use has been removed by the regulation, or not ever if the regulation is to protect the health, environment, or fiscal integrity of the area. Moreover, all of the owner's property interests—lateral and vertical—are considered in evaluating the extent of remaining use after the regulation.[3]
2. What is the remedy for a regulatory taking? Compensation,

even for a temporary taking, because the Fifth Amendment
requires it.[4]

3. Assuming that government has a proper police power rationale for imposing a land-use regulation, what conditions can
   government impose on development? Any conditions that
   bear an "essential nexus" to the proposed use and the problems, if any, that it may cause, which the public/government
   has a right to remedy.[5]

In 1992 the U.S. Supreme Court (USSCT) added substantially to
its analysis of regulatory takings to create a two-part test for decid-
ing when a regulation is an unpermitted taking. It did so in considering three more cases:

1. *Lucas v. South Carolina Coastal Council.*[6] The Court re-
   defined regulatory takings along the lines of the dissenting
   opinion in one of its 1987 cases, significantly increasing the
   likelihood of unconstitutional takings where welfare-based
   regulations like those protecting coastal zones, historic areas,
   and aesthetics diminish private property values.

2. *PFZ Properties, Inc. v. Rodriguez.*[7] The Court declined to
   render an opinion in this case, even after oral argument,
   observing simply that review had been "improvidently
   granted." Thus, it is not clear what level of delay, if any,
   constitutes taking without due process of law under the Fourteenth Amendment.

3. *Yee v. City of Escondido.*[8] The Court decided under what
   circumstances such as rent control (when it acts to substantially devalue landlord's interest in favor of tenant's interest
   in real property) government works a constitutionally protected deprivation of property of the *physical* taking variety:
   none. The Court specifically declined to consider any regulatory taking ramifications.

Lucas: *Of Takings by Regulation and Partial Takings Foreshadowed*

Lucas v. South Carolina Coastal Council is easily the most important case in the 1992 trilogy—if for no other reason than its square

addressing of the regulatory taking issue. In *Lucas*, the Court held (by a six to three majority) that when a land-use regulation takes all economic use from land, it is a taking of property protected by the Fifth Amendment and therefore requires compensation. This is true regardless of the purpose for which the land-use regulation is applied, unless it is to prevent a "nuisance." The Court also suggested that it would find a taking requiring compensation if a land-use regulation resulted in a "partial" taking that frustrated a landowner's legitimate, investment-backed expectations. Finally, the Court suggested it might more strictly require compensation for regulatory takings where land-use regulations were designed to protect historic and aesthetic values and preserve natural features, open space, and views, rather than public health and safety.

The Scope of the Inquiry

Hawaii regulates the use of land more tightly than any state in the nation. The limits of that regulation upon private property are therefore critical to its land policy at both the state and county levels. What follows is an analysis of the application of the "taking" issue after *Lucas* (and *Yee*) to a number of these policy areas, based upon the latest pronouncements on such regulatory takings by the U.S. Supreme Court and how they are likely to affect land policy in Hawaii. These policy areas are:

1. *Open space.* Fully 95 percent of Hawaii's land area is classified in some open space category, with virtually no construction activities permitted except for the occasional residence. Open space recreational uses are permitted in parts of these areas, but even these modest uses are under attack. Under what circumstances can Hawaii continue to forbid economically viable land use in these areas? The *Lucas* analysis is particularly important here.

2. *Exactions, dedications, and impact fees.* A variety of fee exactions and other conditions on land development are typically levied on the land development process in Hawaii, often by means of conditional zoning at the county level, followed by recorded "unilateral" covenants. Others—like 60 percent af-

fordable housing requirements—are imposed by the state as a condition for reclassifying land from one state land-use classification to another. Still others—like Honolulu's proposed per-golf-course fee of $100 million supposedly for low-income housing—lack any written basis whatsoever. The *Nollan* analysis (part of the 1987 trilogy) is important here.

3. *Multistage permitting.* The permitting process at state and county levels in Hawaii averages eight to ten years for multistage projects just to obtain approval to commence development. Even without the variety of exactions and dedications required (noted above in number 2), the process is very long. Whether it is long enough to constitute a deprivation of property without due process of law is not resolved under the *PFZ* nondecision.

4. *Historic preservation and other "welfare" regulations on the use of land.* While Hawaii's state historic preservation law is largely ineffective, many counties have established historic districts under their zoning powers, with heavy penalties for violating strict controls imposed there and in special design districts. The extent to which a two-tier takings test has emerged and what it means for historic, aesthetic, and other largely welfare-based land-use regulations is dealt with tangentially in *Lucas.*

5. *Environmental regulations.* Some regulations are protective of public health and safety; some are protective of the environment, quite apart from human health and safety. Again, the latter are another class of "general welfare" protection regulations. The 1987 *Keystone* decision (another 1987 trilogy case) and the 1992 *Lucas* decision governed what to do with these regulations for the "protection of the environment." The fact pattern in *Lucas* dealt with a state statute designed to protect the coastal zone for both human health and environmental protection reasons.

6. *Downzoning.* What are the rights of government and property owner when land is reclassified from a more intensive use—such as a high-rise apartment—to a less intensive one—such as a single-family residential? Does it make a difference if the owner recently purchased the land at the

more intensive classification? The *Lucas* case suggests the "legitimate investment-backed expectation" standard might apply.

Hypothetical Case Revisited

So how will FEDC fare on its 200 acres of agricultural and conservation land on the ocean? That depends. As the following chapters demonstrate, it probably has a colorable case against the government in at least four areas:

1. It is difficult for government to make a sound argument for keeping all of FEDC's land in what is essentially open space holding zones. If there is no market for agricultural use of the premises, then FEDC has a right to do something else economic on its land. Whether its grandiose resort-recreational scheme is the answer is difficult to say, but some regulatory taking will in all probability be found as things stand—and that will require some compensation.
2. Four years is a long time to be involved in the permitting process, even in a multipermit state and even for a 200-acre mixed-use project as proposed here. It is quite possible that such a delay amounts either to a Fifth Amendment taking under *First Lutheran,* the third of the 1987 takings trilogy, or to a due process taking.
3. Fees and exactions must be authorized by written law (statutes, ordinances, and so forth) and connected by means of a rational or essential nexus to the development upon which it is levied. The alternative is a tax, for which there must be clear and specific enabling legislation. None of Hawaii's four counties has enabling ordinances for impact fees, and all four impose obligations, later recorded as unilateral covenants, on very little written basis. Furthermore, no impact fee or exaction is legal, with or without an ordinance or statute, unless it is designed to ameliorate or eradicate a problem or pay for a public facility, the need for which is generated by the development upon which it is charged or levied. Thus, for exam-

ple, much of the golf course fee is indefensible because it is ad hoc (no ordinance) and because it bears no relationship to the problems caused by, or the public facilities needs generated by, the golf course.

4. Coastal protection is the aim of the shoreline management permit (SMP) issued by the county under the auspices of the state's coastal zone management act. The goals of the act are probably more environment and welfare oriented than health and safety oriented (which is the avowed goal of tsunami inundation zone regulations passed under the auspices of the Federal Disaster Protection Act). While the latter goals are defensible up to a point under the latest trilogy of USSCT cases, the former goals are not.

5. Historic preservation and other clearly welfare-related ordinances are in deep trouble under *Lucas* when they significantly reduce the economic value of private property.

CHAPTER 2

Preserving Open Space

One of the more difficult regulations to justify both philosophically and legally is the preservation of open space through public regulation of private land use. If private property is protected under the Constitution except from taking by due process, for a public purpose, and upon payment of just compensation, then requiring an owner to preserve open land under the police or regulatory power must leave the owner with some viable use and serve to protect the health, safety, and welfare of the people. While it may be easy to justify preventing a landowner from constructing a sugar mill in, say, a residential area, it is vastly more difficult to justify eliminating all structural uses on private property for the sole purpose of preserving open spaces for the public to view or otherwise enjoy. Hawaii nevertheless does so at both the state and county levels. This chapter examines the legal and institutional mechanisms for preserving open space by regulation in Hawaii and analyzes the legal and institutional issues raised by these mechanisms against the backdrop of the 1987 and 1992 decisions of the U.S. Supreme Court.

The Mechanisms: The State

The State of Hawaii preserves open space principally by means of its state Land Use Law.[1] Enacted in 1961 to preserve prime agricultural land from the perceived ravages of urban sprawl on Oahu, the law was also the product of the Democratic revolution in the 1950s, which resulted in a concomitant loss of power by the landholding (and largely Republican) *kamaaina* (native-born or long-time residents).[2] The land-use law is essentially local zoning writ large. An appointed Land Use Commission divided the state into three (and later four) "districts" or classifications by 1964: urban, rural, agricultural, and conservation. The state partially or totally controls the use of land in the last three, which account for at least 95 percent of Hawaii's land area.[3] Only on the small percentage of urban land is development of any intensity (multifamily and single-family residential on lots smaller than half an acre, commercial, resort-residential, industrial) permitted, and then only if the county with jurisdiction over the land similarly permits development.

Agricultural Land and Open Space

The agricultural district includes land used not only for traditional agricultural purposes such as cultivation of crops and grazing, but also for a range of other uses that, with one exception, are largely open space in nature. These include open area recreational facilities, specifically golf courses and driving ranges, on relatively unproductive farmland.[4] The major exception is sugar mills, which are otherwise obviously an industrial use, as anyone who has ever watched one in operation will readily concede. The other structural uses permitted are a combination of agricultural (for example, roadside stands, farm dwellings, and storage/maintenance facilities) and nonagricultural (for example, wind energy facilities and utility installations such as transformer stations, communications equipment buildings, and water storage tanks).[5] In terms of use of land area, it is fair to characterize the agricultural district uses as predominantly open space in nature.

However, for several reasons it is inaccurate and misleading to characterize the agricultural district as principally agricultural. First, the growing of sugarcane and pineapple on plantation-sized acreages is in steep decline, and it may become precipitous in the near future. Increased outside agricultural competition coupled with Hawaii's relatively high wage scales, cost of living (particularly housing) and value of agricultural lands has driven thousands upon thousands of acres out of agricultural production over the past ten years.[6] While there is some potential for growing other crops, much of the land currently classified for agricultural use by the state is not so suited. Moreover, the market therefore is limited, and the record of truck farming as a major industry in Hawaii is not good.

Second, the use of agricultural lands for open space recreational use on a large scale, while not popular, is increasingly common. This is particularly true with respect to golf courses. As noted above, Hawaii's Land Use Law permits the use of agriculturally classified land for golf courses as a matter of right on lands with poor agricultural use characteristics. Moreover, even prime agricultural land is used for golf courses under a special permit process administered by both the state Land Use Commission and the counties.[7] The Hawaii Supreme Court has specifically upheld this special-use process for golf courses even though the Land Use Law singles out golf courses as forbidden on prime agricultural land as a matter of right.[8] Largely as a result of such permitted and special uses, Hawaii has 68 golf courses (nearly half in Honolulu) with another 102 proposed, 27 of which are either under construction or nearly through the state and local approval processes.[9]

These factors and the proliferation of other uses in the agricultural district have led some commentators to conclude that much of the agricultural district has simply become an open space holding zone for nearly half the land area in Hawaii.[10] Clearly many of Hawaii's citizens (and probably a goodly number of its tourists) have come to depend upon the open vistas that such agriculturally classified lands provide. But as the economic viability of agriculture as we now know it fades in Hawaii, it is clear that such large areas cannot continue to be so classified unless other economic uses are permitted within the agricultural district. Aside from the dubious fairness of requiring private landowners to provide large (and free) expanses of open space for public enjoyment, even the present state of the law on regulatory takings will not permit a classification that forbids all economic use of land without some basis in health and safety protection (see discussion of *Lucas* case below). Therefore, it is necessary to consider some alternatives.

The most obvious alternative (one that has served Hawaii reasonably well for the past few decades) is to permit other open space uses either as additional or existing uses of right in the agricultural district. By far the most common of these in the 1980s—and recently the most publicly unpopular—has been the use of agriculturally classified lands for golf courses.[11] This is primarily for environmental and social reasons, though there is some sentiment favoring the saving of agricultural land for the future, despite a state legislature–commissioned report predicting that Hawaii has, by several hundred thousand acres, more land classified for agricultural use than it can conceivably use or need for the next fifty years at least.[12]

The major criticisms levied at golf courses on agricultural land are that they are not consistent, they are an urban use, and they are environmentally unsound. These are difficult arguments to accept. First, the state agricultural district specifically permits outdoor recreational uses in general, and horseback riding, hiking, and day camps in particular. In terms of land use intensity and policy, it is difficult to differentiate a golf course from these uses, even if golf courses were not permitted as a matter of right on marginal agricultural land (which they are). That this use is permitted at all is a concession that it is consistent with whatever the agricultural district has become. Moreover, the principal activity, besides actually golfing, is the growing of and caring for grass, trees, and other plants that make up a golf course. The differences between this and the growing and harvesting of crops is very slight. The urban nature of the golf course itself is difficult to fathom. Clearly it preserves large areas of open space that are—depending upon the nature of the golf course—far more open to the public than the crop-growing plantations that in many cases preceded it. Environmentally, most studies demonstrate that whereas the maintenance of a golf course requires some chemical fertilizers and a certain amount of water, less of either is required when compared with previous crop raising.[13]

This is not to suggest that developments associated with golf courses are necessarily consistent with agriculture. (Though some —like clubhouses—are wholly consistent with other uses currently permitted as a matter of right in the present state agricultural district, such as farmhouses and sleeping facilities for employees.) Clearly, golf course developers who consider ringing the course with single-family residences or building an adjacent resort or condominium complex are proposing a use that is patently urban in nature and must obtain appropriate state and local boundary and zoning reclassifications. This should not and does not, however, convert the hundreds of acres of golf courses into urban uses.

The social issues are more difficult to address. People attracted to what they define as a "rural lifestyle" have testified at more than one hearing on golf course development that they regard such development as intrusive. Many view the golf course as the first step toward urbanization. Indeed, some golf course developers view the golf course as an integral part of either a resort-recreational or upscale residential community.[14] These concerns, however, are or ought to be addressed when the golf course is first proposed. The fact that associated uses may not be agricultural in nature does not detract from the agricultural nature of the golf course itself.

The second alternative is to create a new open space district for nonagricultural but low-intensity and basically nonstructural uses in which outdoor recreational uses such as golf courses would be permitted. Not only would much of Hawaii's presently classified agricultural lands (particularly marginal agricultural land) go into this district, but so would those portions of the state-classified conservation district lands that do not fit into truly conservation/preservation categories (primarily those in the most intensively used subzone, discussed in the next section of this chapter). In fact, the State of Hawaii's Office of State Planning (OSP) has proposed such a classification in the past several legislative sessions, by means of a so-called "LESA bill." Indeed, recent OSP recommendations to the legislature presume the existence of such a new open space district, in which golf courses would be allowed by special permit only but barred from all other districts except the urban district.[15] Such an open space district is a reasonable solution to the need for alternate economic uses for the huge acreages held privately and for which there is shrinking agricultural or other open space uses that are economically viable. It is not clear, however, that golf courses can be singled out in such a district for "special use" treatment if other similar uses (from a land-use perspective) are permitted as a matter of right. Thus, it becomes critical to determine what OSP has in mind in creating this district.

In 1991, after considerable effort and redrafting, OSP intro-
duced a bill that modified the standards applicable to reclassifying
agricultural and conservation lands and created a new open space
district.[16] The purpose of the new district is easily gleaned from the
proposed legislative standards for the Land Use Commission's
guidance in setting administrative standards for classifying land in
the open space district:

> In the establishment of the boundaries of the open space districts, open
> space areas, including but not limited to areas which provide buffer
> areas around communities and residential areas; areas which preserve
> scenic views and provide open space for recreational and aesthetic pur-
> poses; and areas which are not of high value as agricultural or conserva-
> tion resources and are not appropriate for inclusion in the urban or
> rural districts shall be included;[17]

Fair enough, but what will be permitted of right? There's the rub:

> (a) Within the open space district all lands shall be restricted to the
> following permitted uses:
>   (1) Agricultural uses as provided in section 205–4.5;
>   (2) Public and private open area types of recreational uses includ-
>   ing day and overnight camps, picnic grounds, parks, riding
>   stables, *but not including* dragstrips, airports, drive-in the-
>   aters, *golf courses,* golf driving ranges, *country clubs* and
>   overnight camps.
>   (3) Low intensity uses compatible with the purposes of the open
>   space district.[18] (emphasis added)

It is difficult to make a case for lumping a demonstrably nonstructural, open space, and low-intensity use like a golf course or
country club with drag strips, airports, and drive-in theaters, all of
which have additional nuisance-like characteristics (noise, glare,
distraction) virtually absent from golf courses and country clubs.
However, aside from this caveat, the bill would be a reasonable and
reasoned alternative to converting the existing agricultural district
into what it has arguably been for many years: an open space
holding/agricultural district in which open space uses such as golf
courses are permitted, but with restrictions, along with traditional
agricultural uses. Failing to choose one or the other of these alternatives will risk litigation that will almost certainly result in a

finding that restricting unproductive (either economically or physically) agricultural land to agricultural uses is a regulatory taking of property requiring compensation under the U.S. Constitution.

This is particularly true after the *Lucas* decision by the U.S. Supreme Court, discussed in Chapter 1. The case clearly holds that depriving a landowner of all economically beneficial use of his or her property is a constitutionally protected taking of property without compensation. How restricting unproductive agricultural land to uneconomic agricultural uses could be described as nuisance preventing (one of the exceptions to this takings rule) is difficult to understand. While it is conceivable that Hawaii's basic common law principles of property law (another exception) might include statutes like the Land Use Law, common law usually means case law, and there are no Hawaii cases either upholding or striking down the Land Use Law. The temporary uses otherwise permitted will probably not be sufficiently "economic" to justify the regulation either, given that Lucas was also able to make modest economic use of his property even under a "no-build" restriction, and yet the U.S. Supreme Court considered the case one of total economic deprivation requiring compensation. Moreover, even if a court were to agree that the economic deprivation was not "total" and that therefore the square holding of the *Lucas* case did not apply, the Supreme Court also clearly suggested in footnotes that partial takings of sufficient magnitude would also require compensation as takings, using as an example a regulation that rendered a parcel 90 percent economically unviable. Therefore, it is difficult to formulate an argument against a taking by regulation should a landowner find that the only truly economic use of his or her property—for agricultural uses—is no longer economic and that he or she is not permitted to use it for another economic use, whether for a golf course or some other demonstrably remunerative activity.

Conservation Land and Open Space

The conservation district is the second of the two large land classifications by the state Land Use Commission. It consists of both public and private land (some estimate that as much as half is private) and amounts to nearly half the land area of the state.[19]

Controlled exclusively by the board of directors (the Land Board or board) of the Department of Land and Natural Resources, the district originally consisted primarily of forest and water reserve zones (initially named and established as such)[20] and lands for the preservation of historic and scenic areas. These lands were used for conserving wildlife, providing park lands and wilderness and beach reserves, preventing floods, and as "open space areas whose existing openness, natural condition, or present state of use, if retained, would enhance the present or potential value of abutting or surrounding communities, or would maintain or enhance the conservation of natural or scenic resources."[21]

This extensive definition would raise few public policy issues if all, or even almost all, of the land in the conservation district were publicly owned. After all, aside from a governmental duty to manage public lands for public purposes (and here the concept of public trust figures prominently)[22] government can pretty much dictate the use of public lands in any manner it chooses, particularly if that use is restrictive. However, a substantial portion of the roughly two million acres of conservation district land is privately owned. The regulation (by the Land Board) of this land raises substantial "takings" issues under the U.S. Constitution, given the unmistakable legislative intent (as amply documented by the history of the Land Use Law pertaining to the conservation district and the forest reserve lands) to preserve open space for scenic purposes and the progressive tightening of the subzones to increasingly reduce land development potential. This is not bad—indeed, a conservation district sounds very much like a district in which development should be minimized. When nearly half the land in the state is placed in such a district, however (and considering that half the remaining land in the state is classified in an increasingly economically nonviable agricultural district), then the problem of who should bear the principal burden of a virtually development-free classification becomes acute.

The Regulatory Framework

The conservation district is regulated by the governing Board of Land and Natural Resources (BLNR or Land Board) of the Department of Land and Natural Resources (DLNR). The Land Board has by administrative rule divided the conservation district into four so-called "subzones" and permits various land uses in each, all as authorized by statute.[23] Also by statute, these uses may include not only farming and the operation of nurseries and orchards, but also "recreational pursuits" and residential use.[24] There are currently four subzones: protected, limited, resource, and general. Regulations promulgated by the Land Board set out the uses permitted in each.[25] The first two subzones are more or less self-descriptive. The protected subzone is to protect valuable resources in such designated areas as restricted watershed, marine, plant, and wildlife sanctuaries; significant historical, archaeological, geological, and volcanological features and sites; and other unique areas. The primary permitted uses in a protected subzone are research, education, and some recreation as long as no permanent facilities are contemplated. The limited subzone is for areas in which natural conditions restrict human activity (40 percent slopes, flooding, volcanic activity), with timber harvesting and flood control added. The resource subzone adds aquaculture to the list of permitted uses. The general subzone adds very little more "of right": water collection and storage, and transmission facilities. Only in special subzones and by means of conditional permits, variances, and nonconformities are economic uses besides agriculture, forestry, and aquaculture permitted.

First, the special subzones, created in 1978, permit specific projects in the conservation district, such as a college, a nursing home, and a convalescent hospital.[26] Although not common, these subzones are occasionally created.

Second, there is the Conservation District Conditional Use Application (CDUA). The Land Board may permit, upon conditional-use application, virtually any use as long as the use will not result in any significant adverse effects to the environment or conflict with the objectives of the subzone. In the past, the board has approved, under the CDUA permit, not only residential uses but a freeway as well.[27] Right now, the CDUA permit is virtually the only route through which a landowner may build a house on privately owned, conservation-classified land. Such conditional-use permits are heavily conditioned and granted only on land in the general and resource subzones.[28] The conditions are all welfare rather than health and safety related, so the denial of a CDUA permit for a house—the denial of which was a "regulatory taking" under *Lucas*—if that is the only "economically beneficial" use of the property, will be a regulatory taking requiring compensation.

It was not always thus. Earlier conservation district use regulations contained only general and restricted watershed subzones.[29] The earlier general subzone permitted not only cabins and other residences (including camping trailers), but also resorts, hotels, restaurants, and ranches. Thus, portions of Waialae Iki and Hawaii Loa College were constructed on conservation district land.[30] These and other perceived abuses resulted in the elimination of such uses as permitted uses and the increasing reluctance of the Land Board to permit structural uses of any kind (except houses) unless strictly required by the aforementioned nonconforming use language in the applicable statutes. Houses are routinely permitted under CDUA permits.

The Framework Applied

Clearly, in the 1990s the only way a private landowner can obtain permission to construct anything like a residence on conservation-classified land is to successfully obtain a CDUA permit. This should be relatively easy in the general and resource subzones and virtually impossible in the others, always assuming, of course, a landowner is unable to prove nonconforming status as described in the preceding section.

But it isn't always as easy as it should be. In 1987, entitled by statute to build a residence, the owner of an apparently nonconforming lot on Mt. Olomana sought and received a CDUA permit to construct a reasonably large residence. However, the landowner failed to commence construction within the one-year period set out in the permit, then in 1988 further complicated his reapplication process by proposing a substantially more elaborate residential complex. The visibility of the site on one of Hawaii's most sacred mountains resulted in a storm of community opposition and the rejection of his plans for building a three-story house and maid quarters, and within months his second CDUA permit request was revoked for failure to commence construction (which is difficult to do unless plans are approved). Apparently recognizing that there is little legal basis for obstructing some sort of development under the nonconforming language in the applicable statutes, DLNR is reportedly acquiring the property through eminent domain proceedings, arguably the only preservation avenue open to it.[31]

In a second case, a landowner has been denied permission to construct a house on a ridge in Lanikai on the grounds that the permit to do so has been revoked. Permission was originally granted in 1978 without a limit on commencement of construction (apparently because there was no such limit when the application was filed), and both DLNR and the state attorney general's office opined that the permit was valid as long as a dwelling was constructed in accordance with its original terms. However, that limitation later appeared in documents pertaining to a bond and security interests in the property, drafted principally by DLNR. The CDUA permit was accordingly canceled in 1990 for failure to commence construction within one year. After a series of tragicomic affirmances and denials of the existence of the permit, the Land Board voted to acquire the property.[32]

In both examples there was massive community objection to development on exposed (and in one case extraordinarily scenic) hilltop ridges. This is the community's right, and their government has every duty to take direction from that clearly expressed sentiment. The question is how. What if the Land Board had not voted to acquire these two parcels? Is there any way in which the board could defend the denial or revocation of appropriate use permits under the existing law? If not, how could it be appropriately changed?

Conservation and Development: Preservation by Acquisition or Regulation?

There has been a variety of proposals to deal with the problem of residential development on land classified in the state conservation district. Most, however, miss the crucial point: if the sole purpose of prohibiting structural development is to protect scenery, does that represent a proper, much less a legal, use of government police power? Moreover, placing all sensitive lands such as Mount Olomana and the Lanikai ridges into a protective subzone solves nothing with respect to the right to build houses as nonconforming uses under Hawaii statutes. Under the existing law, such houses could be built in any subzone. Contrary regulations issued by the Land Board would be an unauthorized restriction on a statutory right.

The statute itself has been amended to take away the existing right to build a residence on a lot that was held for residential use, and existing nonconforming uses could be phased out or amortized over time, as provided in many zoning ordinances. If there are no economic uses remaining, however, then the issue of the basis for the regulatory scheme becomes critical, since there are no reasonably permitted uses left to balance the use of the police power. The balance then tips in favor of compensation to a landowner for a regulatory taking, since it is difficult to characterize such houses as either nuisances or as uses prohibited under common law principles in Hawaii. These are the only exceptions permitted by the U.S. Supreme Court under *Lucas*.

Open Space and the City and County of Honolulu: The Preservation Zone in Planning and Zoning

The designation of open space districts is not the exclusive preserve of the state. Hawaii's four counties also have created open space districts by plan and regulation in their respective zoning ordinances.[33] Of the four, the City and County of Honolulu provides perhaps the best example for additional analysis because of the breadth and sophistication of the classifications, because of the number of people affected by what Honolulu does in relation to the state's population generally, and because a version of the open space regulations has been the subject of relatively recent litigation. The City and County of Honolulu's jurisdiction extends over the entire island of Oahu as well as the northern Hawaiian islands for land-use purposes.

The Development Plans and Open Space

Honolulu's open space regulations are found in its county-wide development plans (DPs) and its Land Use Ordinance (LUO). Nine development plans are required by the Charter of the City and County of Honolulu to implement a general and policy-based plan for the county. The general plan is specifically required by both the State Plan[34] and the state zoning enabling act.[35] Each development plan must contain a map of the area of the county to which it is applicable, as well as standards and principles for the use of land for residential, recreational, agricultural, commercial, industrial, *open space*, institutional, and "other purposes," and it must identify areas, sites, and structures of historical, archaeological, architectural, or scenic significance. Public infrastructure is also required, together with the desirable sequencing of development.[36] What gives the DPs their teeth, however, is the charter-mandated conformance requirement: "No public improvement or project or subdivision or zoning ordinance shall be initiated or adopted unless it conforms to and implements the development plan for that area."[37] This means that all rezonings must conform to the applicable development plan, often requiring a two-step amendment process (DP, then zoning district) for purposes of land development in low-intensity zones. (This process is explored in greater depth in Chapter 5 addressing land-use processes and the concepts of due process and equal protection of the law.)

The development plans for Oahu (which cover the entire island) divide its land area into twelve districts for land-use planning purposes.[38] By far most of the island is classified in agricultural and preservation zones. While generally coinciding with the state agriculture and conservation districts respectively, some of these areas are in the state urban district, which means that the state at least regards these areas as suitable for development. The restrictions on permissible development in the preservation and agricultural planning districts are understandably severe: uses in preservation districts are limited to open space–related uses (crop production, forestry, golf courses, game preserves, livestock grazing, outdoor recreational facilities); uses in agricultural districts don't include many more (farm dwellings and livestock production facilities). After all, the purposes of these districts are to preserve agriculture and various natural features, not to promote development.

The plans themselves don't restrict development; the zoning regulations that must conform to them do. Obviously, Honolulu may not permit, by zoning, uses that are more intense than the area's development plan would allow, either by reclassifying the property to a more intense zone or by approving a subdivision for land development purposes. This is the purview of the Land Use Ordinance.

Zoning and the Preservation of Open Space: The Land Use Ordinance

Honolulu implements its development plans through a comprehensive amendment to its local zoning ordinance called the Land Use Ordinance. Effective since late 1986, the LUO is a complex and sophisticated local land-use code in which virtually all uses of any consequence pass through some sort of administrative review before (and if) they are approved. (This is discussed in Chapter 5 on administration, timeliness of approvals, and due process.) The LUO divides Oahu into thirty-three general and special land-use districts[39] of which the preservation districts are the most important for purposes of preserving open space. But while the state zoning enabling act grants the counties specific authority to designate areas where agriculture and forestry "may be conducted" and general authority to "restrict certain uses" particularly bordering watercourses, there is no mention of preserving open space or undertaking conservation of any sort.[40] The LUO, however, specifically states that a major purpose of the preservation district is to "preserve and manage open space."[41]

Nevertheless, the LUO states that "[t]he purpose of the preservation districts is to preserve and manage major open space and recreation lands and lands of scenic and other natural resource value."[42] The most restrictive of the preservation districts is P-1. What lands will be so classified? According to the LUO, all lands within the state-designated conservation district, over which the county has no control anyway under the state's Land Use Law. Authority over that district is solely in the hands of the state Department of Land and Natural Resources, as noted earlier in this chapter. The LUO acknowledges this by stating that all uses, structures, and development standards in the P-1 district will be governed by "appropriate State agencies."[43]

This leaves the P-2 general preservation district. Actually there is quite a list of permitted uses in this district, ranging from crop production, forestry, and grazing to outdoor recreational facilities (golf courses?), public uses and structures, and cemeteries. Moreover, zoos, waste disposal facilities, and vacation cabins are conditionally permitted uses under certain circumstances and after administrative reviews. Of course, minimum lot sizes of five acres somewhat reduce the utility of vacation cabin uses, for example, given land prices in Hawaii, particularly in Honolulu.[44]

What is the likely effect of classifying substantial parcels of land in the P-2 preservation category? This was an issue for the Hawaii Supreme Court in *Kaiser Development Company v. City and County of Honolulu*.[45] There, in the first of more than a dozen lawsuits challenging the "downward" reclassification of private property pursuant to the newly promulgated development plans for Oahu and the concomitant zoning reclassifications conforming to these plans, the court resoundingly upheld the theory and practice of the development plans and the zoning behind them by refusing to recognize either a taking or a right to compensation when Honolulu reclassified private property from a designation permitting construction of a resort hotel (and at one point residences only) to P-2 preservation.

Would this be the result today? The size of the parcel together with the poor nature of the soil would make agriculture, forestry, and grazing remote possibilities. Its beachfront location would make it largely unsuitable for public utilities or solid waste disposal, and five-acre minimum lot sizes would make it financially impractical to build vacation cabins on the site. One logical alternative might be a golf course (if that is included in the outdoor recreational permitted use), but local politics being what they are, this may not be a viable alternative either. Thus, one could easily conclude that the property has little, if any, viable economic use.

Given that the purpose of the classification is clearly related to public welfare rather than health or safety, it will undergo the strictest of judicial scrutiny to see whether a regulatory taking has occurred.

Conclusion

It is difficult to see how many of the avowedly open space classifications in Hawaii will survive the heightened judicial scrutiny resulting from *Lucas* and its progeny. The classifications are clearly public welfare in nature, cast as they are to protect views and other natural resources entirely divorced from human health and safety. Therefore, the public purpose justification is legally weak. Worse, there are virtually no economically beneficial uses permitted, depending of course on the location and acreage in particular cases. As the disputes over residences in state conservation district lands clearly demonstrate, government will be increasingly forced to purchase private land to preserve many of these areas. Because of the costs involved, such purchases will not be common. Without them, however, successful challenges to the regulations must surely result.

The problem of open space use becomes particularly acute as the prospect of large state reclassifications from the agriculture to the conservation districts looms prominently. Acting under the five-year land-use district boundary review mandated by the Land Use Law,[46] OSP has recommended to the Land Use Commission the reclassification of thousands of acres of agriculturally zoned land, much of it privately owned, into the conservation district.[47] Many ranchers, particularly on the neighbor islands, vigorously oppose such a reclassification and have threatened to challenge them in court as regulatory takings. The rationales for the reclassifications as suggested by OSP range from watershed preservation to protection of habitats.[48] How these will fare under *Lucas*, particularly if DLNR (which will control land use on the reclassified lands) restricts present agricultural practices (such as grazing), remains to be seen.

The answer is to permit a range of uses compatible with open space preservation in all but the most scenic and resource-laden areas. A case can be made for preservation where—as is common —there are severe natural site limitations on development in such locations as mountaintop, hillside, and beachfront. These fit well into the *Lucas* "nuisance" exceptions. For the rest, eminent domain is a limited but viable alternative. For the vast majority of the areas now classified in agricultural, conservation, or preservation districts, a new district is a necessity, at least at the state level. All state land classified as agricultural and conservation that is not either used or clearly usable (practically and economically, not theoretically) for agricultural purposes, or needed for watershed, or naturally site-limited should be placed in this zone or district, with viable (though limited) economic uses permitted, such as golf courses, vacation cabins, and sensitive rural-resort and residential uses, with tight limitations to preserve as much as possible the open space character that the public really wants. Otherwise, there is a need to recall Justice Holmes's dictum in 1922: "a strong desire to improve the public condition is not enough to warrant achieving the desire by a shorter cut than the constitutional way of paying for change."[49]

CHAPTER 3

Preserving the Built Environment

Most people in Hawaii would agree that saving historic buildings, cultural sites, and land-based artifacts is an important goal. Many would further agree that government should help attain it. Enthusiasm for the conservation and preservation of this "built environment," however, is often in direct proportion to whether or not the preservationist owns the property in question. Most would agree that government ought to preserve significant buildings, sites, and so forth, that government owns. The national brouhaha over the conservation of the Gettysburg battlefield, where Union and Confederate armies fought one of the most significant battles in the Civil War, serves as one of the better examples. Although there is some dispute today over how certain federal lands should be used (open space vs. grazing; timber production vs. endangered species preservation), much of the built environment in government hands generally remains intact, if not as well-preserved as some would like. At best, the issue becomes one involving notions of public trust, absent specific statutory direction to conserve and protect.

Privately owned structures and sites raise different issues. There are essentially three elements to the preservation of these structures and sites: regulation (to prevent damage and destruction), rehabilitation and reuse, and protection from federally funded development. Of these, regulation raises the most policy issues.[1] In light of increasingly common experience, together with the recent decision by the U.S. Supreme Court in *Lucas* (see Chapter 1), conservationists and preservationists must increasingly turn to the second (and to some limited extent, the third) element in order to protect the built environment without running a significant risk of taking property by regulation without compensation.

Regulation and Preservation

The basis for regulating these aspects of the built environment is the same as for zoning and other forms of land-use control: the police power. Most would accept that there is little basis for resting such preservation on the health and safety legs of the police power. This leaves, once more, the welfare clause. In historic preservation, cultural artifact preservation, and architectural preservation, the issues are much the same: what is the basis for requiring a private landowner to preserve, largely if not exclusively at his own expense, structures that the public deem important? Does it make any difference what criteria the public uses to decide what should be preserved and what should not? Do "compensable regulations" such as the transfer of development rights solve the takings problem? Before delving into these issues, let's first explore what Hawaii does to preserve historic and cultural and architectural icons at the state and county levels.

Historic Preservation and the State: Strong Principles, Weak Practice

The State of Hawaii is in a particularly strong position to protect historic and cultural sites because of the language in Article IX, Section 7, Constitution of the State of Hawaii: "The State shall have the power to conserve and develop objects and places of historic or cultural interest and provide for public sightliness and physical good order. For these purposes private property shall be subject to reasonable regulation." Pursuant to this broad mandate, the state has enacted a historic preservation program of sorts that deals with publicly and privately owned historic sites. There are many statutory requirements dealing with the proper use of public historic sites and artifacts. While important, the issues they raise deal largely with the care and husbandry of public resources. The regulatory scheme that governs the use of *private* historic sites raises the kind of regulatory takings issues discussed in the *Lucas* case.

On private lands, the relatively recent authority conferred on the state historic preservation officer to review all projects affecting historic properties is the most significant authority that the state exercises by statute. Until DLNR gives its "written concurrence," no such project may be "commenced, or in the event that it has already begun, continued."[2] While the applicable state statute appears at first to apply only to state projects, the statute defines project in such a way as to apply to private developments that need a permit or "land use change or other entitlement for use" either from the state or "any of its political subdivisions."[3]

The effect is to subject virtually any development project to DLNR review. If the concurrence of DLNR (through its historic preservation officer) is not forthcoming, then the "agency or officer" seeking to proceed with the project can "apply" to the governor who "may" request an advisory council on historic preservation to report or take action as the governor deems best in overruling or sustaining DLNR. Moreover, state and local government agencies are under an obligation to report the finding of any historic property during any "project" and cooperate with DLNR in its "investigation, recording, preservation and salvage[.]"[4] Presumably under this section, the construction of a private office building was delayed for more than a year after the demolition of a city parking structure while experts pored over unearthed artifacts dating back to the nineteenth century.

Still of some importance is the statutory process of listing historic sites on the Hawaii Register of Historic Places. This registration is the responsibility of the Historic Places Review Board (which also recommends sites for the National Register of Historic Places, to be discussed later). The appointed ten-member board acts in accordance with statutory criteria.[5] Before construction, alteration, disposition, or improvement upon such a listed property, the landowner must notify DLNR and permit a review. If DLNR concurs, or if ninety days elapse from the date of notification without action, then the owner may commence whatever he had planned, unless the state first condemns the property or undertakes the aforementioned investigation, recording, preservation, or salvage.[6]

Finally, a historic site may be subject to Hawaii's Environmental Policy Act (HEPA or HEIS), which requires an environmental impact assessment and potentially a full-blown environmental impact statement. HEPA is triggered by any "proposed use within any historic site" listed on either the Hawaii or National Register of Historic Places.[7] Of course, once an assessment or environmental impact statement (EIS) is completed, the landowner is free to proceed with the project (see preceding paragraphs).

Historic Preservation by the Counties

Historic preservation from a regulatory perspective continues strongest at the county level. State statutes specifically grant to counties authority to regulate, by planning, zoning, or other regulations or special conditions or restrictions, both historic properties and "adjacent or associated private property" for their protection, enhancement, and preservation, both with respect to *appearance and use*. Moreover, counties may regulate by other means, including historic easements (presumably by purchase or condemnation) and transfer of development rights.[8] This is pretty strong stuff. Even before this relatively recent statutory addition, many counties enacted historic preservation district provisions under the power granted to them by the state zoning enabling act.[9]

The City and County of Honolulu's use of the special district to regulate for historic purposes is one of the more draconian uses of local land-use controls. Separate special districts are created in the LUO of Honolulu for the state capitol, Chinatown, Thomas Square, and the Honolulu Academy of Arts, and Haleiwa, the boundaries of which are graphically portrayed at the back of the LUO.[10] No development is allowed in these districts without a special permit from the director of the Department of Land Utilization (DLU). The permits are issued only in accordance with strict criteria listed in the text of the LUO for each district. There are criteria for building height, landscaping, and architectural appearance and character, dealing with everything from architectural form to exterior wall materials, colors and facades, and in some instances "street" furniture and railings.[11]

Each of the state's counties is also directed to review and issue special management area (SMA) permits under the state Coastal Zone Management Act in accordance with various objectives, one of which is to protect, preserve, and restore natural and man-made historic and prehistoric resources that are significant in Hawaiian and American history and culture.[12]

Architectural Controls: Aesthetics Again

Architectural controls are increasingly common methods of land-use control in the United States. While there do not appear to be any state statutes in Hawaii dealing with them, this has not prevented Hawaii's counties from passing laws protecting architectural features. The use of architectural controls to protect historic districts in Honolulu was noted in the preceding section. Honolulu's LUO also controls architectural features by means of special districts for design purposes only, wholly apart from historic preservation. It does so for Diamond Head, Punchbowl, Waikiki, and the state capital.[13]

The special district for the state capital is perhaps the most instructive. Among the objectives are the preservation, protection, and enhancement of structures and the safeguarding of buildings that "represent or reflect elements of the State's civic, aesthetic, cultural, social, economic, political and architectural heritage."[14] There follows a list of street corridors and specific buildings deemed particularly worthy of attention, such as the Hawaiian Electric Building, the YWCA, St. Andrew's Cathedral, and the Royal Brewery. As all of these are private buildings, restrictions on their use must pass the U.S. Supreme Court's regulatory takings tests. And restrictions there are. No building, structure, or landscape element is permitted, and no additions, demolitions, removals, or relocations are allowed unless the purpose is to restore an exterior (in an appropriate manner), or to comply with other specific architectural requirements, or to improve the function of private and public structures and spaces.[15] Other design districts provide for the establishment of design advisory committees to advise the DLU director on the permitting process applicable to that special district.[16]

Preservation Policy and the Law

Community preference for preserving what exists against the ravages of new and often alien development is neither new nor surprising.[17] However, as Dean John Costonis has observed, the law can do no more than provide a framework for preservation; it is wholly unsuited to provide actual standards for what is worth preserving, let alone what is beautiful.[18] The USSCT attempted to do this in 1978 in *Penn Central Transportation Co. v. City of New York*.[19] Admittedly unable to define a "bright line" across which strict regulations were unconstitutional takings of property, the Court nevertheless declared that the police power basis of the regulation coupled with its effect on the legitimate investment-backed expectations of the property owner were factors to consider. The Court also clearly recognized that the welfare clause was an appropriate basis for regulation, depending always on the effect the regulation has on private property. Whether this test remains viable today for preservation cases is, of course, open to debate, in light of either the 1987 or the 1992 takings cases. In any event, the Court upheld New York City's denial of permits to Penn Central for the construction of a multistory office building over the historically listed Grand Central Station, mainly on preservation grounds. The Court did so by recognizing that preservation and aesthetics were proper police power purposes under the welfare clause. But it upheld the regulations largely because it found there were other existing and potential economic uses for the terminal building. Not only did the Court find that the existing use was profitable, but it also found that by either transferring the unusable "development rights" above the terminal to nearby property owned by the railroad[20] or by applying for a smaller building above the terminal (which was originally designed for such an addition), Penn Central could be additionally "compensated" for its inability to build a larger building for historic preservation reasons. As noted in the preceding section, a state enabling statute permits the counties to use transfer of development rights as a compensatory regulation device to preserve historic and cultural sites, but to my knowledge this power is so far unexercised by the counties.

Notwithstanding the language in *Penn Central* supporting preservation regulations under the welfare clause of the police power, such regulations have fared poorly in the past few years in the courts. First, courts have begun to carve out exceptions to the proposition that preservation regulations are broadly acceptable when first amendment rights are threatened. This has been particularly true when the designation of religious buildings are perceived to threaten the First Amendment guarantee against interference with religious worship.[21] Second, courts have struck down designations of historic buildings when the interference with private property rights is deemed too great. Thus, the Pennsylvania Supreme Court recently struck down the designation of both the interior and exterior of a theater in Philadelphia over the objection of the landowner. The court reasoned that Philadelphia was forcing the owner to bear a public burden (to enhance the quality of life in Philadelphia as a whole) for the benefit of sightseers and the public at large—a burden that should be borne by all, not just the landowner.[22]

When the language in *Lucas* is coupled with the suggestion in a decision by the California courts on assessing whether a taking had occurred in one of the famous 1987 Supreme Court trilogy cases,[23] there are dark days ahead for the preservation movement, whether historic, cultural, or aesthetic. In the California case, the court suggested that it was taking its cue from the Supreme Court in postulating separate tests for regulations based on the health and safety legs of the police power and for regulations based on the welfare leg of the police power. The court suggested that it would be substantially more inclined to find a regulatory taking when the effect on private property was less than full destruction of economic rights, if the basis for the regulation were welfare based. On the other hand, if it were health and safety based, then the court would be more likely to require that substantially all economic use be gone from the private property so regulated before finding a regulatory taking had occurred. The language in *Lucas* tracks this sort of analysis by disparaging the use of the police power to confer public benefits, particularly when beneficial economic uses of the property suffer.

Preservation by Use and Reuse: An Alternative to Regulation

An alternative to addressing the difficult policy and legal alternatives posed by preservation through regulation is the use of non-police power methods to achieve the same goal. The encouragement of use and reuse of historic and other sites and buildings worthy of preservation on a national scale commenced when certain federal tax incentives, since largely withdrawn, were made available for developers of historic sites in the early 1980s. The concept survived, however, in many parts of the United States,[24] particularly in Hawaii.

Sometimes the encouragement for historic preservation comes not through government regulation or incentives, but from communities themselves. Such a situation occurred within the community of Haleiwa. This community is situated within the Haleiwa scenic design district. Set between the contrasting backdrops of sugarcane fields and the rugged surf of the north shore, Oahu's Haleiwa long has been known for its unique seaside-country character. Local residents interested in preserving this rural character focus their efforts through an organization called Haleiwa Main Street.

In 1990, in response to increasing and sometimes hazardous traffic on the portion of Kamehameha Highway that passes directly through the town of Haleiwa, the state of Hawaii began a revision of the highway route, which would then bypass the town of Haleiwa. Faced with having the majority of the visitor traffic bypass the town completely, the community chose to protect its local interests and the character of its town through a rather risky endeavor. With its own funding, Haleiwa Main Street hired a consulting firm to assist in the development of a conceptual plan for Haleiwa. The purpose of the conceptual plan was to map out ways that Haleiwa could compensate for the lost business resulting from the highway bypass while preserving the town's character.

After gathering extensive input from local residents, the final conceptual plan reflected the community's desire to preserve the historic rural character of the town while promoting tourism and business to counteract the effects of the highway bypass. After receiving approval from the Design Advisory Committee, Haleiwa convinced the city council to approve the concept of the plan.

Conclusion

The State of Hawaii has increased considerably the authority of the state's counties to regulate private property to preserve historic, cultural, and other sites. In this it has the support of the Constitution of the State of Hawaii. Clearly, counties such as Honolulu have for some years now heavily regulated private land in certain special districts for historic and aesthetic purposes, all now permitted under state enabling statutes, and these regulations apply to churches as well as business buildings, specifically. Moreover, statutory directives under coastal zone management and environmental impact laws also provide a layer of protection for historic and cultural sites.

But it is also clear that such regulations may have constitutional problems at the federal level, and that many state supreme courts around the country are so holding both on First and Fifth Amendment grounds. Moreover, there is a strong suggestion that all built environment preservation laws will be under far stricter judicial scrutiny, based as they are on the welfare leg of the police power rather than the more traditional nuisance-related health and safety legs.

This leads to the conclusion that going about preservation through encouraging the use and reuse of the aesthetic, historic, cultural, and architecturally significant built environment is likely to be both more defensible and more satisfying. In this, Hawaii is a national leader.

Exactions and Development Conditions: Impact Fees, Development Agreements, Golf Courses, and Housing

Fueled by a growth rate exceeding planned expectations, many attractive areas of the country have been unable to meet the demand for new public facilities such as roads, sewers, water, schools, and parks. Explosive growth has also exceeded the resources for affordable housing. Local governments—traditionally the providers of these facilities—have found to their chagrin that traditional sources of funding for such facilities have failed them just as the need has increased. The federal government has vastly reduced the funds available to local government for public works. New taxes on new development often comes too late, and increasing property taxes (the basic source of funds for local governments for generations) is either politically unpopular or illegal. Special assessments generate revenue only from the area surrounding the facility, are statutorily complicated to do, and again are usually too late.

Consequently, many local governments have turned to exactions or conditions upon the land development process to help pay for those public facilities that growth and development make necessary. Curiously, the basis for such conditions or exactions is not the power to tax, but the power to regulate, the police power that is a natural attribute of sovereignty. The reasoning goes that since most public facilities are for the health, safety, and welfare of the people, the method of paying for them specifically (as contrasted with a general revenue levy or tax that targets no particular facility or purpose) is an exercise of the police power. This is a critical distinction, since local government needs specific authority from state government through specific enabling statutes to levy taxes, but it may generally levy exactions, conditions, or impact fees on the land development process under general authority to regulate land (zoning) and the land development process (subdivision or development codes). Most local governments have these powers. Certainly all four of Hawaii's counties have such general authority.[1] Consequently, most statutes specifically "enabling" impact fees actually limit or condition local government's preexisting power to collect impact fees.[2] The 1992 Hawaii state impact fee legislation is no exception, containing many conditions as discussed below.

Legal and Policy Basis for Exactions

The exaction, charge, or condition on the land development process essentially takes three forms:

1. *The development exaction or in-lieu fee.* This is usually a requirement that a land developer construct and dedicate roads, parks, school sites (occasionally school buildings), and similar public facilities within the boundaries of a development project or, if the project is too small to warrant a major facility, contribute cash "in lieu" thereof.
2. *The impact fee.* This is a requirement that developers pay a fee toward the construction of a regional public facility such as a wastewater treatment plant, major road, sewer system, or solid-waste disposal site that will serve their development and others, usually to be located outside the boundaries of their particular development.
3. *The zoning condition.* This is a requirement usually in the form of a fee payment, sometimes in the form of an "up front" dedication or contribution, which depends on the granting of a zoning change or major permit. Conditional zoning is a common form of such zoning conditions.

While much of the recent case law dealing with such conditions and exactions has developed from challenges to the impact fee, the language is applicable to all three. To be enforceable and valid, an impact fee must be levied upon a development to pay for public facilities, the need for which is generated, at least in part, by that development.[3] This is the so-called "rational nexus" test developed by the courts in Florida and other jurisdictions that have considered such fees and exactions.[4] First proposed in 1964,[5] it became the national standard by the end of the 1970s.[6]

The test essentially has two parts. First, the particular development must generate a need to which the amount of the exaction bears some roughly proportionate relationship. Second, the local government must demonstrate that the fees levied will actually be used for the purpose collected.[7]

This test was confirmed and made applicable to all land development conditions by a decision of the U.S. Supreme Court in 1987. Decided on the last day of the Court's 1987 term, *Nollan v. California Coastal Commission*[8] deals ostensibly with beach access. Property owners sought a coastal development permit from the California Coastal Commission to tear down a beach house and build a bigger one. The commission granted the permit only upon condition that the owner give the general public the right to walk across the owner's backyard beach area, an easement over one-third of the lot's total area. The purpose, the commission said, was to preserve visual access to the water, which was impaired by the much bigger beach house. The Court, however, held that, assuming the commission's purpose to overcome the psychological barrier to the beach created by overdevelopment was a valid one, it could not accept that there was any *nexus* between these interests and the public lateral access or easement condition attached to the permit:

> It is quite impossible to understand how a requirement that people already on the public beaches be able to walk across the Nollan's property reduces any obstacles to viewing the beach created by the new house. It is also impossible to understand how it lowers any "psychological barrier" to using the public beaches, or how it helps to remedy any additional congestion on them caused by construction of the

Nollans' new house. We therefore find that the Commission's imposition of the permit condition cannot be treated as an exercise of its land use power for any of these purposes.[9]

However, the Court said, it is an altogether different matter if there is an "essential nexus" between the condition and what the landowner proposes to do with the property:

> Thus, if the Commission attached to the permit some condition that would have protected the public's ability to see the beach notwithstanding construction of the new house—for example, a height limitation, a width restriction, or a ban on fences—so long as the Commission could have exercised its police power (as we have assumed it could) to forbid construction of the house altogether, imposition of the condition would also be constitutional. Moreover (and here we come closer to the facts of the present case), the condition would be constitutional even if it consisted of the requirement that the Nollans provide a viewing spot on their property for passersby with whose sighting of the ocean their new house would interfere. . . . The evident constitutional propriety disappears, however, if the condition substituted for the prohibition utterly fails to further the end advanced as the justification for the prohibition. . . . [T]he lack of nexus between the condition and the original purpose of the building restriction converts that purpose to something other than what it was. The purpose then becomes, quite simply, the obtaining of an easement to serve some valid governmental purpose, but without payment of compensation. Whatever may be the outer limits of "legitimate state interests" in the takings and land-use context, this is not one of them.[10]

Cases decided in state and lower federal courts after *Nollan* make it clear that the nexus test for land development conditions of any variety is now the law of the land.

How does this analysis apply to Hawaii? Essentially, Hawaii makes use of impact fees, conditional zoning, and subdivision exactions. The use of the first two, together with housing linkage requirements, raises legal and policy questions in the context of the *Nollan* decision and its aftermath.

Impact Fees and Golf Courses: Nexus Bogied

The importance of the rational nexus requirement in levying impact fees is difficult to overstate. First, most recent cases setting out the rational nexus test requirement are impact fee cases.[11] Second, impact fees are by definition charged for regional facilities that only partially benefit each landowner charged a portion of the cost. Third, the public facility will almost certainly be located off-site rather than within the landowner-payor's contemplated development project. Fourth, the landowner will almost always pay cash rather than construct a facility in order to satisfy his or her development condition when it is in the form of an impact fee, since each landowner is paying only a proportionate share of the cost of the facility that their combined land developments make necessary. For example, a solid-waste disposal site costing millions of dollars may well be paid for through a combination of impact fees charged to several landowners together with general tax revenues. Its location will depend only marginally on proximity to the development sites, as long as it is in the general area of the proposed development.

There are several other important factors for local governments to consider in levying impact fees:

1. They may be, and usually are, used for off-site public facilities.
2. They can be, and usually are, collected from a number of developer-landowners, usually at the building permit or subdivision approval stage of land development.
3. They are collectible even if the public at large is a primary beneficiary, as long as the landowner-developer derives some benefit and the contribution is in proportion to that benefit.
4. They should be collected for facilities to be constructed in accordance with some sort of public facilities plan.
5. The money collected must be segregated into an account for that particular facility (roads for roads, sewers for sewers, and so forth) and spent as soon as possible, or the need for the facility, and hence the fee itself, becomes questionable.
6. The use of benefit zones in which the facility will be constructed and from which land the fees will be collected is a useful device to assure an appropriately rational or essential nexus.[12]

Among the caveats:

1. The fees must be charged as a part of the land *development* process, not the land reclassification or rezoning process. Fees are development-driven, and land reclassification, while it may well be a prelude to development, does not create any need for public facilities whatsoever.
2. Collected fees do not belong in the general fund, or once again the need becomes questionable.
3. The fees cannot be kept by government for years and years, for the same reason stated in number 2 above.
4. While there is no need for an enabling *statute*, impact fees cannot be levied without an *ordinance* reducing much of the above to a written law. Ad hoc charges are questionable on grounds of both law and policy. The development community and the public are entitled to know the rules of the land development process, and they must be fair, uniform, and based on clearly articulated plans and standards.

Ignoring the foregoing raises a presumption, as a matter of both law and policy, that the impact fee is nothing more than a revenue-raising device, either for a facility that has nothing to do with the land development upon which the fee is raised, or for undetermined fiscal purposes generally. In either case, the "fee" is then presumed to be a tax. This characterization as a tax is almost always fatal to an impact fee, since most local governments have very little specific authority to tax beyond the property tax and, occasionally, a sales or income tax. Since an impact fee is neither of the above, and since all local government taxes must be supported by specific statutory authority, the fee is almost always declared illegal.[13]

This does not mean, however, that the impact fee itself must be specifically enabled in a state statute. Although several states have such statutes,[14] most state courts that have considered the issue find ample authority in the general planning and land development control authority granted most local governments, together with statutes giving them general responsibility for water, sewer, schools, roads, and so forth.[15] Indeed, the result of enabling legislation in some states has been to drastically cut back the authority of local governments to charge impact fees for many types of public facilities.[16] This appears to be one of the purposes behind the 1992 statute that requires Hawaii's counties to formulate and pass impact fee ordinances. Not only are the fees limited to certain subjects (pointedly and specifically excluding lower income housing), but also a number of specific "credits" for other developer exactions are deducted from fees owed.[17] The fees also must be preceded by a "needs assessment study." This would be particularly unfortunate, given the vast range of facilities for which fees are used throughout the country, as Table 1 shows.

Impact fees would appear to be ideally suited for a sunbelt growth state like Hawaii. There is a need for public facilities largely because of growth and land development. Hawaii's four counties have limited financial means to pay for such facilities; they certainly lack many tax alternatives. Moreover, the counties have development plans that contemplate where development and the accompanying necessary public facilities should go, even if all are not as clearly defined as the public facilities element of the Honolulu development plans. The counties most certainly have adequate enabling statutes, and most have clear responsibility for developing various public facilities categories as well.[19]

It is both fair and practical to have the land development community pay its proportional share of the cost of such facilities. Indeed, many already do, as discussed in the following section, in an ad hoc (and arguably unsatisfactory) method of enforced contributions with little basis in law and less in policy. Strangely, with two glaring and patently illegal exceptions, the counties have no ordinances by which to exercise the legal authority they have to levy impact fees.[20] Therefore, as a matter of law they lack authority to levy any impact fee whatsoever. Hopefully, the 1992 legislative directive to the counties to formulate and promulgate such an ordinance will soon result in such ordinances.

The statute is particularly important given the ongoing debate over the use of impact fees to both regulate and tax the development of golf courses in Hawaii. This is not the appropriate forum for engaging in a lengthy exposition on the advantages and disadvantages of golf course development, already the subject of several government-sponsored studies and reports.[21] Moreover, Chapter 2 argues that golf courses are an appropriate use of open space under

Table 1. 1991 National Average Impact Fees by Type[18]

Type of Impact Fee	Single Home per Unit	General Industry	General Office	General Retail
		(per 1,000 square feet)		
Road				
Low	$ 16	$ 41	$ 79	$ 200
High	7,782	5,210	16,500	36,063
Average	1,567	1,364	2,141	3,268
Park				
Low	50	130	130	130
High	12,000	1,688	1,688	1,688
Average	1,035	702	715	703
Public Facility				
Low	49	7	57	57
High	7,169	12,000	12,000	12,000
Average	910	1,385	1,447	1,481
Police				
Low	14	8	8	8
High	933	520	520	520
Average	120	68	110	111
Fire				
Low	21	1	3	3
High	2,500	1,000	1,370	2,400
Average	217	157	204	244
Library				
Low	30	90	90	90
High	238	150	261	158
Average	130	118	167	133
School				
Low	135	250	250	250
High	3,160	280	280	280
Average	2,663	259	259	259
Water				
Low	60	30	30	30
High	11,660	50	104	62
Average	1,225	37	55	41
Sewer				
Low	40	60	60	60
High	9,405	1,440	1,440	1,440
Average	1,558	750	750	750

(continued)

Table 1.   (*Continued*)

Type of Impact Fee	Single Home per Unit	General Industry	General Office	General Retail
		(per 1,000 square feet)		
Total				
Low	415	617	811	828
High	54,847	22,538	34,163	54,611
Average	9,425	4,858	5,848	6,990
Less Water and Sewer				
Low	315	527	707	738
High	33,782	21,048	33,519	53,009
Average	7,642	4,071	5,043	6,199

NOTE: These averages originate from the 206 local governments participating in this survey.

several scenarios. The issue here is whether the levy of a so-called impact fee of up to $100 million per golf course, variously proposed by the mayor of the City and County of Honolulu[22] and (at substantially smaller figures but still running into the millions of dollars) the city council,[23] is defensible.

The answer is clearly no. First, there is yet no ordinance, statute, or other law that permits the charging of such a premium. Second, there is no demonstrable connection or nexus between such huge sums of money and any public facility that Honolulu expects to build with the money, which is related to the development of golf courses. It may very well be that golf courses generate a need for roads and sewers and water improvements, but the general collection of millions of dollars under the guise of an impact fee without connecting the money to the need is neither good policy nor good law. Third, the only purpose so far mentioned by the city (largely through the mayor) for such a premium is affordable housing. The need for such housing is, as noted later in this chapter, clear and unambiguous, but the connection between golf course development and that housing need is not. What possible housing needs does a golf course generate? If golf courses generate such a need, how about shopping centers (a federal court in California upheld such a low-income housing connection in 1991),[24] hotels, resorts, and other commercial developments, which at least generate large numbers of entry-level jobs for which housing may be needed near-by? There is no basis for conditioning the approval of golf courses on the payment of any fee whatsoever without some sort of ordinance, and then only if the fee is rationally or essentially related to a public facility need generated by the proposed golf course.[25]

Conditional Zoning: Reclassification/Development

Conditions on rezoning and conditions on development proceed from different bases in law and policy. The purpose of placing conditions on the land reclassification or rezoning process at common law is to prevent the use of land in a fashion that would be inconsistent with the overall zoning scheme or development plan for the area. Honolulu specifically provides for conditions on rezoning in its LUO.[26] Before the enactment of a zone change, the LUO specifically provides that the city council may impose conditions on the applicants' use of property. The reasons are to protect the public from "potentially deleterious effects" of the proposed use and to fulfill the need for "public service demands created by the proposed use."[27] The LUO then provides that the required conditions be formally recorded in a so-called "unilateral agreement."[28] This is a fundamentally flawed process for at least two reasons. First, there is no reason why the two purposes set out in the LUO cannot be accomplished by other more traditional and defensible means. Providing for infrastructure and public facilities is the business of the development or subdivision exaction or impact fee, discussed in the preceding section. Protecting the public from deleterious effects of a use is usually accomplished either by removing the use from the zoning district or by making it a special or conditional use, approved according to strict standards and by permit only by a zoning administrative officer after a hearing, but without a zone change. Second, the method of memorializing the conditions—the unilateral agreement—is both illegal and a contradiction in terms, because there is no such thing as a "unilateral" agreement that is enforceable. An agreement presumes at least two parties, and to be enforceable something called "consideration" must flow both ways. In other words, each party must obtain something in order for it to be enforceable.

There are also more general problems with Honolulu's practice. Related to or often treated the same as contract zoning, the practice of conditional zoning comes dangerously close to bargaining away the police power of local government, which without a statutory basis, as for development agreements (discussed in the next section), is generally illegal in most jurisdictions.[29] Moreover, it is difficult to know what is or is not permitted in a mapped zone classification if zoning approvals are regularly hedged with conditions on approval, such as the common one of limiting the existing uses to fewer than those permitted in the new zone classification under the local zoning ordinance.[30] Such limitations rarely have anything to do with the appropriateness of the use in the district. Rather, community and/or government opposition—either to most of the uses permitted in the zoning ordinance in that district or to the particular use, without conditions governing how the use is to be carried out—are among the salient reasons for conditioning the rezoning. If the concerns are legitimate, then perhaps the controversial other uses should be removed from the zoning classification as uses "of right" and permitted only upon certain articulated conditions, thereby leveling the playing field for all participants in the zoning game. Otherwise, the zoning ordinance itself becomes something of a *shibai* (pretense).

A more insidious condition on rezoning has nothing to do with the land-use effects of the proposed use itself, but everything to do with the value of the rezoned property after reclassification. An exaction or fee is charged at the reclassification stage, usually on the ground that the public has somehow become entitled to share in the value that accrues to private property upon its reclassification. Most recently, Honolulu has charged landowners a fee or premium equal to 25 percent of the increase in expected value after reclassification or rezoning. Thus, if land were valued at $10,000 prior to rezoning and $20,000 after, the city would charge the landowner $2,500. This premium is based on the notion that the public has created the value and should therefore benefit from it. The premium is half of the "windfalls for wipeouts" equation popular in the 1960s in England and the 1970s in the United States.[31]

However, that equation is badly flawed on three counts. First, as with impact fees and exactions in Hawaii, there is no legal basis for imposing the premium, and there is no written ordinance, written regulation, or statutory basis upon which to pass or promulgate one. Second, there is no nexus—rational, essential or otherwise— to impose such a condition on the rezoning process even if there were such a written law. Recall that exactions such as impact fees are development driven, made necessary in order to pay for public facilities for which new development generates a need. Rezoning may well be a prelude to development, but it does not yet begin to trigger public facilities needs. Indeed, the rezoned land may be changed to a less intense classification (or "downzoned") later, as happened to many parcels of land throughout Oahu when Honolulu's development plans became law in the mid-1980s. Third, the equation is inconsistent. If landowners have to pay for windfalls, then they are entitled to compensation for wipeouts or reductions in property values that result from public land-use decisions as well. Does Honolulu propose to pay landowners compensation for that reduction in value, or will it (rightfully) argue that much of the downzoning was necessary for the health, safety, and welfare of the community? To charge a premium for reclassifying land for more intense use, or "upzoning," is a tacit admission that such reclassification is for other than the health, safety, and welfare of the people, which strikes at the legal and policy foundations of zoning. If there is an increase in value to the landowner associated with that change, then the public will benefit through increased real property tax collections. Otherwise, the public has no business skimming value that has accrued to individual owners through a public decision on land use that has presumably been made in the interests of the public as a whole. The charge is either an illegal impact fee (no ordinance, no rational nexus) or an illegal tax (no enabling statute).

State Exactions: Housing Exempted?

The State of Hawaii also attaches conditions to land use. When the Land Use Commission undertakes boundary amendments— zoning writ large—particularly from the agricultural or conservation districts to the urban district, it often attaches conditions to the reclassification. Because there is a statutory basis for many of these conditions, they are both legally and institutionally more sound than those imposed by the counties, discussed in the preceding sections. This is in part because of the many directives contained in the Hawaii State Plan, which is itself a statute, and in part because of the responsibilities assigned to the Land Use Commission by its own enabling legislation, the Land Use Law.[32]

Act 100 was mentioned briefly in Chapter 2. Essentially, it directs Hawaii's major land-dealing and regulating agencies (DLNR, the Land Use Commission) to act in conformity with its overall themes, goals, objectives, and policies, and to use its priority guidelines (along with the state functional plans approved by the governor).[33] Act 100 sets out goals, objectives, policies, and guidelines for population, economy, agriculture, visitor industry, federal expenditures, potential growth, physical environment (land-based, shoreline, marine, scenic, natural beauty, historic, land, air, water quality), facility systems (transportation, water, solid and liquid wastes, energy/telecommunications), housing, health, education, social services, leisure, culture, public safety, government, individual rights, and personal well-being. The Land Use Commission is also directed to consider the impacts of any proposed reclassification on certain "areas of state concern" having to do with the preservation of natural systems, maintenance of cultural and historic resources, maintenance of agricultural resources, commitment of state funds, employment and economic development, and housing opportunities for all income groups, particularly low, moderate, and gap.[34]

Housing is a useful example of how an agency such as the Land Use Commission would be guided in making its boundary amendment decisions, in part because of the explicit nature of Act 100, and in part because of the commission's controversial policy during 1988–1991 of requiring a set-aside or quota of so-called "affordable" housing (as high as 60 percent) as a condition for boundary amendments to the urban district for residential development purposes.

Act 100 sets out the following objectives for housing, to which decisions of the Land Use Commission must conform:[35]

1. Greater opportunities for Hawaii's people to secure reasonably priced, safe, sanitary, livable homes located in suitable environments

that satisfactorily accommodate the needs and desires of families and individuals.

2. The orderly development of residential areas sensitive to community needs and other land uses.

In order to achieve these objectives, Act 100 sets out the following policies, to which Land Use Commission decisions must conform:

(2) Stimulate and promote feasible approaches that increase housing choices for low-income, moderate income, and gap-group households;

(3) Increase homeownership and rental opportunities and choices in terms of quality, location, cost, densities, style, and size of housing;

(5) Promote design and location of housing developments taking into account the physical setting, accessibility to public facilities and services, and other concerns of existing communities and surrounding areas;[36]

Priority directions the Land Use Commission must consider in making its decisions are not particularly directed toward the regulatory framework in which the commission works, with the exception of the first one: "Seek to use marginal or non-essential agricultural land and public land to meet housing needs of low and moderate-income and gap-group households."[37] The directive of the Land Use Law, however, is to consider the impact of a proposed classification on "Provision for housing opportunities for all income groups particularly the low, low-moderate, and gap groups."[38] Taken together, these statutory provisions would probably be sufficient for the Land Use Commission to use the mandatory set-aside of affordable housing units as a condition of reclassifying land to the urban district from any other classification, for the purpose of residential development. Indeed, they would probably be sufficient for such reclassification for any urban purpose, all things considered, especially when one of the things to be considered is the mix of housing that would make up the 60 percent affordable figure. In the past, such a percentage has included housing at very nearly market rates, as well as a substantial percentage at the decidedly low end of the market. As noted before, as of early 1992 the Land Use Commission had either suspended or abandoned the policy of such mandatory set-asides, at least in part because there were no petitions before the commission for re-classification and in part because some residential developers who had agreed to such conditions were finding it too difficult to construct any sort of housing in the existing (1992) market if the affordable quotas were adhered to.

However, while these statutory provisions clearly give the Land Use Commission not only the authority but the responsibility to undertake policies such as mandatory set-asides in order to address Hawaii's housing problems, this does not mean these provisions are necessarily constitutional. Just because the State of Hawaii declares there is a nexus between the construction of market housing and the need for affordable housing does not necessarily make it so. The few cases that so far have considered such "linkage" requirements have either upheld housing fee or set-aside requirements on *commercial* developments that were expected to attract low-income wage earners (and so arguably have an obligation to provide housing for them if none was otherwise available—a federal court in California split over whether implementing a "social policy" like housing needs is a proper subject for exactions),[39] or upheld them as part of an already articulated and thoroughly developed local obligation to accept regional fair-share housing needs pursuant to state constitutional requirements.[40] Neither of these circumstances fits the Land Use Commission's mandatory set-aside of a full 60 percent of affordable housing units. The chances of such a high figure being ruled a taking of property without compensation, especially when grafted upon a housing (rather than a commercial) development at a very preliminary land classification (as opposed to land development) stage, are substantial, particularly in light of the language in the *Nollan* case requiring a nexus.

Statutory Development Agreements: The Exactions Problem Resolved

There are two problems with the way that Honolulu and, to some extent, the state go about extracting community benefits from landowners: lack of legal authority and lack of essential nexus.

Either there is insufficient legislation at the state and/or county level to support an exaction, condition, or impact fee, or they are charged at a level or for a purpose that is prohibited. The solution to both problems is the statutory development agreement, which is already provided for by statute and is consensual in nature, not a police power exercise. Therefore, no nexus test—rational, essential, or otherwise—is applicable to it.

The development agreement is a contract between a unit of local government and a landowner. The principal purposes of a development agreement are to guarantee a landowner contemplating development that at least some of the land-use and development laws applicable to his or her property will not change during the land development process, and to guarantee to government that the landowner will provide various public benefits beyond those that government could legally require through the police power. In short, the purpose is to vest certain development rights in the property owner in exchange for payment, construction, or dedication of public facilities, low-income housing, and the like.[41] The development agreement is particularly attractive to developers of multiphase projects, or in multipermit jurisdictions such as Hawaii, where new rules and regulations on the land development process may evolve either between phases or before sufficient action in reliance on existing permits occurs to "vest" the landowner's right to proceed with a project. The attraction to government is the legal ability to obtain more community benefits than it could require through exactions and impact fees. For example, a recent 500-page development agreement in California between San Francisco and Catellus Corporation for mixed-use development on Mission Bay provides for the following community benefits:

—$4 million for 250 units of "very low income" off-site housing;
—2,000 housing units with 740 affordable units within ten years;
—865 affordable on-site housing units;
—68 acres of park and open space;
—26 acres of clean, improved affordable housing land to city;
—$12.9 million and 3 acres for community/cultural facilities;

—$85 million and land for infrastructure (streets, utilities);
—$24 million transit impact development fee;
—$9.3 million school impact fee;
—$6.1 million child care fee;
—$5.3 million for public art;
—$10 million for economic development fund; and
—$2.25 million for public health.[42]

Since it is often stated that local governments cannot usually "bargain away the police power" or otherwise bind future legislative bodies,[43] most states promoting the use of development agreements have provided for them by statute.[44] Typically, the statutes recite the public purposes that have led the state to provide for development agreements, set out the process for negotiating them, list the bare-minimum subjects a development agreement must address (usually use of land and bulk standards such as building heights), limit the duration of the agreement or provide that the agreement must have an ending date, provide specifically that those land development regulations in effect at the time of the development agreement remain in effect during its duration unless imminent hazard to health and safety require unilateral modification by local government, and provide for mutual extension or modification.[45] This is the pattern of the Hawaii development agreement statute passed in 1984.[46]

Unfortunately, only one[47] of Hawaii's four counties so far has passed an ordinance setting up local procedures for development agreements, arguably a requirement of Hawaii's statute, which came from California. This is apparently due to vocal opposition from a variety of public interest groups opposed to development agreements on the grounds that they will be privately and secretly done, contrary to good planning practices. Neither argument is accurate, of course, since the state statute requires a public hearing on any negotiated development agreement and forbids the inclusion of any provision contrary to existing development plans. The opposition in Hawaii is even more puzzling, since California, from which Hawaii took much of its statute, has seen the signing of hundreds of development agreements in hundreds of cities and counties since 1980, so far without a single lawsuit challenging them.[48]

Moreover, California has since amended its development agreement statute to specifically remove local government ordinance requirements as a barrier.[49] A recent report by the Hawaii OSP recommends this or a similar amendment to permit the negotiating of statutory development agreements without the need for such ordinances as a prerequisite.[50] Of course, any county may choose not to negotiate a development agreement with any particular landowner.

In sum, the development agreement is an excellent tool, clearly authorized by statute in Hawaii, for government to negotiate community benefit packages to obtain for the public many of the facilities for which government can no longer pay, and which it may not legally require as a condition of land development—including affordable housing.

Housing the "Other Way": The "Projects" of the 1990s

Affordable housing is clearly a major issue in Hawaii. Median housing and condominium prices are estimated to have increased from $140,000 to over $350,000 and $85,000 to about $190,000, respectively, between 1980 and 1990. During the same period, rents for apartments, condominiums, and townhouses went from $500 to $1,150 per month. Rental vacancy rates hover at 1 percent, and the number of households on waiting lists for federal rent assistance alone rose from about 2,700 to nearly 7,000 between 1982 and 1991. The number of homeless rose a staggering 500 percent during roughly the same period.[51]

Hawaii provides most of its housing assistance not by set-asides and exactions but by direct government intervention—an older, more traditional, and arguably more successful way to help solve Hawaii's obvious housing crisis. The agencies providing such programs are the Hawaii Housing Authority (HHA), the Hawaii Community Development Authority (HCDA), and the Hawaii Housing Finance Development Corporation (HFDC). Of these, HFDC has been the most active in the past half-dozen years.

Carved out of HHA in the early 1980s, HFDC pursues its housing assistance goals through a number of mechanisms, but its most important (and potentially most successful) goal is its role as master developer. Essentially, it acquires raw land, puts in infrastructure, and partners the actual housing development with the private sector. For example, this process enabled HFDC to recently sell single-family detached homes in Kapolei for $110,000, though they cost an estimated $154,000 to construct and carried an appraised value of $275,000.[52] In order to preserve the affordability of its units, particularly those for sale, HFDC uses a combination of right of first refusal and shared equity. Thus, during the first ten years following initial occupancy, an owner-occupant who wishes to sell a unit must first offer it to the state at a predetermined price. Thereafter, the state shares in the sales price (earlier if it chooses not to repurchase during the initial ten years), acquiring much of its initial equity investment, with the difference going to the homeowner.

HFDC works primarily through three master-planned communities divided into several villages. The first of these communities is Kapolei, in Ewa. Eight villages are to be constructed on approximately 900 acres acquired from the Estate of James Campbell, after the investment of $27 million in infrastructure. Approximately 60 percent of the units constructed will be "affordable" (120 percent of the median income on Oahu, or below). So far, about 500 units have been completed and occupied, with 600 more in the construction stage in two of the villages and 300 to 500 units to be constructed in five additional villages. Additional communities are planned on Maui (4,300 units over twelve to fifteen years) and the island of Hawaii (4,200 units), with a mixture of single-family, multifamily, and rental units. The total for all three communities is expected to reach 13,000 dwelling units. This represents just under one-quarter of the estimated 64,000 affordable units needed by the turn of the century.

Conclusion

In sum, impact fees and exactions—indeed all conditions on land-use approvals—must clearly meet a nexus test in order to be validly levied. Moreover, they must be levied on the process of development and not on the process of land reclassification. The latter may in fact raise the value of the property rezoned, but this causes no public facility or other infrastructure needs. It is at best a taxable event, for which a tax may be levied, but only if there is statutory authorization for such a statute. Presently, there is no authorization at the county level, nor have the counties successfully passed impact fee ordinances pursuant to state statute. Counties are currently without power to do more than exact relatively mild conditions on subdivision approvals, though they continue to do so with impunity. Obviously, many such exactions are in all likelihood unconstitutional takings of property without compensation under the *Nollan* case.

An obvious and statutorily authorized method of obtaining the myriad community benefits and needs not legally connected to a particular development is the development agreement. Indeed, a major report by OSP urges the use of the development agreement for major developments.[53] California's experience with such agreements is long (over ten years) and positive (no reported cases challenging over six hundred such agreements now in effect or expired). However, even the development agreement will not solve Hawaii's housing crisis, and mandatory set-asides and exactions, tied as they are to the land development process, are slow, inefficient, and chancy. HFDC points the way to successful public intervention in the housing market by providing the impetus for hundreds, and soon (hopefully) thousands, of units annually to be constructed at "affordable" rates, though until present demand is met, perhaps the period during which the state has the first option to buy back the units could be indefinitely extended beyond ten years so that the unit is not lost to the affordable housing stock. This may be hard on the occupying family, which may find itself stuck in subsidized housing for a longer time than if it could simply sell the house and "trade up," but the housing problem has reached crisis proportions, and such problems demand tough solutions—provided they are legal.

"Ordinary Delay": Due Process and Land-Use Permitting Process in a Multipermit State

Delay in the land-use permitting process is inevitable. Too much delay is expensive for both private and public sectors. It is also unconstitutional. Just how much delay is permissible? In 1987 the U.S. Supreme Court suggested, for example, that "normal" delays in the rezoning process would not be considered "temporary takings" of property requiring compensation.[1] However, extraordinary delay in processing requests for permission to develop land was the basis of a case before the court in 1992.[2] While the court ultimately decided not to review the decision, it nevertheless accepted briefs and heard oral arguments. The landowner sought money damages and orders of the court permitting him to proceed with his project on the grounds that years of delays constituted denial of equal protection of the laws and due process of law—both constitutional allegations that, if proved, result in takings—as well as damages under the Civil Rights Act.[3]

The problem of delay has raised substantial policy issues for years, entirely aside from the constitutional issues noted above. Experts and other commentators have railed against the delays permeating the land development process and have suggested all manner of "permit simplification" schemes to alleviate them.[4] Sometimes the delay results from the sophistication and complication of the land development process.[5] Other delays are the result of purposeful local government action to temporarily halt development either while new planning or regulatory controls are developed and implemented (the ubiquitous development moratorium), or while the local government decides how and where to proceed with a public facility. Thus, for example, a California landowner lost an opportunity to lease her land for mineral development while a county government kept her land in a "reservation" zone as it contemplated using it for a landfill.[6]

Hawaii's multilayered land development permission process is particularly vulnerable. Estimates vary, but many agree that it can easily take seven years "from blueprint to bulldozer," particularly if the land to be developed needs to be reclassified under state and county land-use laws.[7] Whether such a time period is justified under the due process clause, as suggested in the *PFZ* case (see Chapter 1), is not at all clear. Moreover, it is a substantial waste of time, often translating into higher costs for the ultimate product, whether house, store, or factory. Indeed, some state legislators and county officials are so convinced that the regulatory process adds unnecessarily to the cost of housing in Hawaii that they seek to "fast-track" affordable housing projects by reducing processing time to two years in order to help cut the ultimate cost.[8] Therefore, a close examination of what the U.S. Supreme Court has said about due process and land-use and development permissions, and how selected Hawaii processes measure up, is worthwhile.

The Legal Climate: Defensible Sophistication or Delaying Sophistry?

The basis for a due process challenge to the land development permitting process essentially comes from *First English Evangelical Lutheran Church of Glendale v. County of Los Angeles.*[9] There, the U.S. Supreme Court suggested that delay in the land development approval process might be a taking of property under the Constitution. In this case Los Angeles County refused to permit a church to rebuild a youth camp on a site that had been recently flooded. The sole issue the Court had to decide was whether compensation was an appropriate remedy for a regulatory taking (the Court said it was), not whether the refused permit amounted to such a taking. However, the majority opinion contained some language from which taking circumstances might be implied. For example, after observing that the posture of this case required the Court to assume that all use of the church's property had been taken by regulation, the Court said: "[O]f course [we] do not deal with the quite different questions that would arise in the case of *normal delays in obtaining* building permits, changes in zoning ordinances, variances and the like which are not before us."[10] (emphasis added) The implication that an extraordinary delay would be a taking in the eyes of the Court is inescapable, particularly when the quoted language is set beside the Court's holding that money damages are an appropriate remedy for a "temporary taking" (at least if it is a total taking of property) as well as for a "permanent" one.

Development Permits in Hawaii: What Result, and Why?

Hawaii's development permit process is easily among the most complex and time-consuming in the fifty states.[11] In Hawaii's multipermit jurisdiction, a landowner intending to develop land classified by the state in either the conservation or agricultural districts (95 percent of the state, as compared to less than 5 percent in the urban district, which permits the counties to decide land use by ordinance without much state review or control) must begin with the state Land Use Commission and then go to the county in which the land is situated for reclassification and a variety of land-use permissions. What follows is a summary of the most salient requirements, to illustrate why land development permits often require several years of process before even a modest project is ready for construction.

State Permission: Reclassification and Special Permits

Recall that only in the state urban district are lands designated ripe for development by the state Land Use Commission. While permissive only (the county makes the decision about where and what kinds of developments will be permitted within the urban district), the urban district contains those lands that are currently in urban use, together with a reserve for urban growth. The counties, by 1991 amendment, also have the power to "further define" "accessory" agricultural uses in the agricultural zone, such as golf courses, farm buildings, mills, and roadside stands.[12] Whether such "definition" would allow a county to say where such permitted uses may go in a district, or whether it could eliminate them entirely, is an interesting question in absence of a definition of "define." This is no idle question, as at least one of the state's four counties has taken the position that it may keep golf courses out of state-classified agricultural districts where the state statute clearly declares them to be a use which "shall" be permitted.

It is also possible that uses not traditionally agricultural in nature may be permitted in the agricultural district by means of a special permit. By statute, such uses must be "unusual and reasonable." Application for special permits in this district are filed with a county agency (the planning commission in the neighbor islands, DLU in Honolulu), which may by rule establish procedures and time limits for holding a hearing. If the proposed use is greater than fifteen acres, the Land Use Commission must also approve, and the county agency must send its decision (and record of proceedings) to the commission within sixty days. The commission itself then has forty-five days to act.[13]

If the use is not one permitted as of right, and if a special permit is not forthcoming either from the county or the Land Use Commission,[14] then a landowner needs a boundary amendment reclassifying the property in the urban district, after which the landowner will need to go to the appropriate county for further permissions, as described in the next section of this chapter. The boundaries of the state's four district classifications are reviewed at least every five years as a matter of legislative policy. Often this review results in reclassification. Aside from this required five-year review, any government agency and any "person with a property interest" in land can ask for reclassification. If the parcel is less than fifteen acres, the appropriate county may hear and decide the application, unless the land is in the conservation district. Reclassification petitions for parcels over fifteen acres (and all reclassification requests in the conservation district) go to the Land

Use Commission. The commission must conduct a hearing on whatever island the property happens to be 60 to 180 days after a landowner petitions it. There are detailed statutory requirements for notice of the hearing, and certain county and state agencies are required as parties to the proceedings. Virtually anyone else affected by the process may also be parties if they wish, and the commission must "freely" permit virtually anyone else who wishes to intervene to do so. In particular, community group representatives must be heard. The length of the hearing and the number of times it may be continued are not limited. Whenever it ends, the commission must make its decision within 120 days.[15]

If the proposed development is in the state conservation district, then once again a boundary amendment before the Land Use Commission is required unless the relatively stringent special or conditional use permits (CDUA) will do for a minor development. As noted in Chapter 2, not much development is permitted of right in the conservation district. However, golf courses have been permitted by means of the conditional use permit process, depending upon the subzone in which the subject property is classified or reclassified. The process is generally regarded as "one-step" but can be a lengthy and time-consuming one. A hearing before the Land Board at a specially convened meeting for the purpose is required for any use in a protective subzone, and for any "commercial" (such as a golf course) use anywhere in the conservation district. Hearings must be scheduled within 180 days of a completed application or the use is deemed granted. However, there are a number of submissions required for a complete application, and the time period does not commence running until such completion.[16] Continuations and postponements are not uncommon. Obviously, even this "one-step" process is likely to take a minimum of six months and has taken as long as several years. Thus, a CDUA permit was issued for a golf course with "accessory" uses in 1987 at Koolaupoko on Oahu,[17] and at Salt Lake in 1965.

Clearly, for a golf course developer one of the advantages of seeking such a CDUA from the Land Board is the avoidance of lengthy additional land-use approval processes at the county level, as described below. This appears to be part of the rationale behind occasional petitions to reclassify land from the state agricultural district (generally perceived as a less restrictive classification) to the state conservation district (generally perceived as a more restrictive classification) by prospective golf course developers. While this makes good "permit simplification" sense, it is, of course, questionable whether the use of conservation district land for a golf course, let alone its "accessory" uses, represents a proper use of conservation lands. Once again, a fifth state land-use classification permitting such recreational uses as a matter of right (discussed earlier in Chapter 2), would be helpful.

Protecting the Environment: HEIS, Coastal Zone, and Clean Water

State processing of land development permissions in Hawaii does not end with the boundary amendment procedures described above. The need to protect our fragile island environment has led to a variety of regulatory regimes applicable at both the state and county levels, all relatively uncoordinated, and that add substantial time to the processing of land development applications. Designed primarily to protect particularly fragile environmental areas both inside and outside the state conservation district (described above and in Chapter 2), these regulatory frameworks require additional permits and formal evaluations that result in far more than "normal delays in obtaining changes in zoning ordinances."[18]

Environmental Impact Assessment: HEIS and Its Forbears

The explosion of substantive environmental laws (clean air, clean water, and so forth) in the 1970s was preceded—barely—by the statutory notion that federal actions having the potential for adversely affecting the environment should be subject to some sort of compulsory review—hence the birth of the National Environmental Policy Act, or NEPA.[19] NEPA requires the preparation of an environmental impact statement, or EIS, for every major federal action significantly affecting the quality of the human environment. Each EIS must contain a detailed statement by the "responsible federal official" on the environmental impact, unavoidable adverse environmental effects, alternatives to the proposed action, irreversible commitments of resources, and the relationship between local short-term uses and long-term productivity. "Actions" include funding of federal programs and proposed legislation. An explosion of litigation in federal courts immediately followed the passage of NEPA, in which virtually every phrase describing the requisite contents of the mandatory EIS was subject to painstaking judicial scrutiny. Oddly, a finding of dire environmental consequences fails to stop a project under NEPA; it requires disclosure only.[20] In Hawaii, NEPA litigation over the future of the H-3 freeway in the 1970s delayed the commencement of construction by several years.

NEPA only applies when the federal government is somehow involved, however, and few private land development proposals trigger that involvement. It is the Hawaii version of a state environmental protection act that has the greatest impact on private development projects in Hawaii because of the breadth of development activity it includes. Designed to pick up where the federal law leaves off, HEPA requires not an impact *statement* but an impact *assessment* whenever an action proposes

—any use of land in the state conservation district;
—any reclassification of state conservation district land;
—any shoreline use;
—any use in a historic site designated either nationally or by the state;
—any use in the Waikiki special district;
—any amendments to county general plans by a private party proposing a development designation;
—any use of state or county lands or funds.[21]

The environmental assessment is prepared by a governmental agency for the purpose of determining whether a full-blown EIS along the lines of those required under NEPA should be required upon a finding that the proposed action may have a significant effect on the environment. Both the assessment and, if necessary, the EIS must be made public. The government then decides whether or not to "accept" an EIS depending upon whether it is complete and procedurally sound. There is no provision for rejection on the grounds that it discloses adverse environmental consequences.

Clean Water Permit Requirements: 404 and 402

As with many states and local governments, Hawaii is subject to land development permitting processes based upon federal environmental protection statutes. Among the most applicable to Hawaii land development are the federal permit requirements based on the Clean Water Act.[22] Of these, the most important in Hawaii is the authority of the Army Corps of Engineers to require permits for the discharge of dredged or fill material into the navigable waters of the United States, including wetlands.[23]

Corps-permitting jurisdiction extends to waters of the United States, including but not limited to mudflats, wetlands, wet meadows, sloughs, and sand flats. Wetlands are defined as areas inundated or saturated by surface or groundwater at a frequency and duration sufficient to support a prevalence of vegetation typically adapted for life in saturated soil conditions. They generally include swamps, marshes, bogs, and similar areas.[24] Most discharges require permits unless they relate to agricultural or forestry activities, are determined to be *de minimis,* or constitute runoff or nonpoint sources as compared to point source discharges. Dredged and fill materials are otherwise broadly defined so that virtually any construction activity in a wetland area or activity likely to result in discharge into a nearby wetland or navigable water of the United States will require a Corps permit.[25]

The permitting process is usually directed by a district engineer (one of twelve under the supervision of a chief engineer for the Corps). The process broadly requires the following:

1. Preapplication consultation with the district engineer;
2. Detailed application form usually requiring certification of compliance with other programs such as coastal zone management and water quality.

3. Determination by district engineer that the application is complete within fifteen days of filing; more time allowed if the district engineer concludes the application is incomplete;
4. Publication of notice of the proposed project;
5. Comment period following number 3 above, for interested parties/other agencies, fifteen to thirty days from notice of proposed project;
6. Public hearing, which anyone may request during the comment period and which the district engineer must hold unless he or she determines that the issues raised are insubstantial or that no valid interest would be served by a hearing, (usually holds hearing);
7. Decision within sixty days of completed application unless long hearing, extensions, as noted above.

This permit review is not limited strictly to the natural environmental effects of the proposed project on wetlands and navigable waters. The Corps also undertakes a "public interest review," which balances a broad range of environmental and economic factors, specifically including aesthetics, land use, and historic properties, as well as energy needs, mineral needs, and food/fiber production.[26] The point of the review is that wetlands are important to ecosystems, and their unnecessary destruction is contrary to the "public interest." Moreover, certain wetlands—set aside for study, or that serve significant natural biological functions, shield other areas from flooding, or are necessary for drainage—perform significant public functions, and the Corps will not permit their destruction without significant alternate benefits.[27] The list of specific public interest values upon which the district engineer must consider the effect of a project is long and varied:

wild and scenic rivers, historic properties and National Landmarks, National Rivers, National Wilderness Areas, National Seashores, National Recreation Areas, National Lakeshores, National Parks, National Monuments, estuary and marine sanctuaries, archeological resources, including Indian religious or cultural sites, and such other areas as may be established under federal or state laws for similar and related purposes.[28]

Of course, the district engineer may deny a permit resulting in a discharge that will have an unacceptable effect on the aquatic eco-system without reference to a public interest review.[29] The Environmental Protection Agency (EPA) also has the power to veto a permit decision under alternate sections of the Clean Water Act.[30] Finally, other agencies, such as the U.S. Fish and Wildlife Service (FWS) and the National Marine Fisheries Service (NMFS), may request administrative appeals of Corps decisions to the assistant secretary of the Army for Civil Works. Figure 1 is a summary of the process.

Also, any party proposing to discharge any pollutant into a waterway must obtain a permit from either the federal government or a federally certified agency under the National Pollution Discharge Elimination System (NPDES).[31] Since intensive use of land anywhere in Hawaii is impossible without some provision for sewage and other waste disposal (usually in waterways), the administration of this federal program is another critical permit process. In Hawaii, an application is filed with the Department of Health no less than 180 days prior to the expected discharge of pollutants. After making a tentative evaluation, including tentative effluent limitations and a compliance schedule, the state health director publishes public notice and provides for a thirty-day comment period. Upon petition of another agency or interested group or person, the director considers whether it is in the public interest to hold a hearing before issuing the permit.[32]

The County: Traditional but Additional

While the State of Hawaii has a vast array of land-use permitting processes, as described above, the control of land use for the purposes of land development is still primarily a county function, through development plans, zoning ordinances, subdivision or development codes, and shoreline management for coastal zone and flood hazard protection.[33] This reflects a national condition, for while there has indeed been a "Quiet Revolution" in land-use controls at the state level, the *ancien régime* of local control has not so much been overthrown, or even superseded, but more or less overlaid.[34] In Hawaii in particular, the result has been a sophisti-

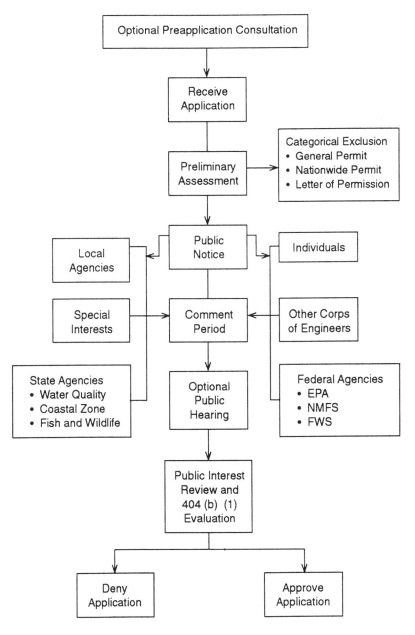

SOURCE: Adapted from U.S. Army Corps of Engineers

Figure 1. U.S. Army Corps of Engineers Permitting Process

cated but complicated and time-consuming process that more or less takes up where the state processes leave off—at least with respect to the Land Use Commission and boundary amendments. While the counties may well classify state urban-classified land in their own open-space planning and zoning classifications (as noted in Chapter 2), the greater tendency is to plan and zone it for development, which is what the state has in mind with the urban district.

County Zoning: The Honolulu Land Use Ordinance and Planning

In 1986 Honolulu replaced its venerable and much-amended Comprehensive Zoning Code (CZC) with the more general and flexible LUO. The product of planners rather than lawyers, the LUO is easier to comprehend, but more difficult to apply. There are fewer landowner "rights" and vastly more administrative discretion in the permitting of land use. There is also more administrative review of proposed uses, and more power concentrated in the hands of zoning administrators like the director of DLU and the chief planning officer, head of the Department of General Planning (DGP). Nevertheless, in its broadest sense, the LUO is a local zoning ordinance that divides the island of Oahu into zoning districts with permitted, special, and conditional uses under each, and accompanying bulk, parking, and other land-use standards. The rest of the LUO text—and there is a lot—consists of administrative provisions governing the permit process.

The LUO first divides Honolulu into twenty-six regular (and eight special) land-use districts, on twenty-four zoning maps.[35] An example is the resort district, shown in Table 2, with principal permitted uses in the first column, permitted accessory uses (besides those in Article 9 of the LUO) in the second, and uses permitted only under certain conditions in the third. Bulk "development standards" are shown in Table 3. If a use is not permitted as a principal, a special accessory, or a conditional use, then it is not permitted on land classified as "resort" on the zoning maps, and some sort of change, most likely a change of zone classification to another of the twenty-six regular zones, would be necessary. As

Table 2. Resort District Permitted Uses and Structures

Principal	Special Accessory	Conditional
Art galleries, museums	See Article 9, Accessory	See Article 4
Bars, nightclubs, taverns	Use	*Conditional uses, Type 1:*
Cabarets, dance halls		Helistops
Commercial parking lots and garages		Historic structures, use of Joint development
Convenience stores	In addition:	Joint use of parking
Dwellings, multifamily	Amusement and recre-	Marina accessories
Eating establishments	ation facilities, indoor	Off-site parking facilities
Golf courses	Business services	Utility installations, Type
Hotels	Day-care facilities	B
Meeting facilities	Duplex units	
Public uses and structures	Dwellings, detached, one-	
Recreation facilities, out-	family, two-family	
door	Financial institutions	*Conditional uses, Type 2:*
Telecommunications an-	Home occupations, see	None
tennas, provided that	also Article 3	
fencing or other bar-	Kennels, see also Article 3	
riers are provided to	Medical clinics	
restrict public access	Personal services	
within the area ex-	Photography studios	
posed to a power den-	Retail establishments	
sity of 0.1 milliwatt/ cm^2		
Time sharing		
Theaters		
Transient vacation units		
Utility installations, Type A		

SOURCE: Land Use Ordinance

discussed below, the Honolulu City Council is ultimately responsible for such a change. However, Honolulu requires conformity to site-specific development plans (a critical preliminary step) before such a "rezoning" request can either be initiated or adopted.

Development Plans: Consistency and the Annual Review

While the local zoning ordinance governs the use of land in most cities, counties, and villages in the United States, Hawaii is one of

Table 3. Resort District Development Standards

Standards	Resort
Minimum lot area	15,000 square feet
	There shall be no minimum lot area for off-site parking facilities
Minimum lot width and depth	70 feet
	There shall be no minimum lot width or depth for off-site parking facilities
Yards	
Front	25 feet
	Except for necessary access drives and walkways, all front yards shall be landscaped
Side and rear	20 feet
	Within 10 feet of the property line, yards shall be maintained in landscaping, except for necessary access drives and walkways
	For duplex lots, 5 feet for and portion of any structure not located on the common property line; the required side yard is 0 (zero) feet for that portion of the lot containing the common wall
Optional yard siting	Parking lots and garages may extend to side and rear property lines, provided the following requirements are met:
	1. An area or areas of open space equivalent to the area to be used for parking or accessory use structures is provided elsewhere on the zoning lot. This open space shall be maintained in landscaping, except for drives or walkways necessary for access to adjacent streets. Parking may overhang the open space up to 3 feet if wheel stops are installed. A minimum of 50 percent of the open space shall be contiguous to the street frontage abutting the zoning lot.
	2. Any parking floor in the 10 feet adjacent to the property line shall not be more than 4 feet above existing grade.
	3. Landscaping required under Section 3.80 of this Chapter is provided and maintained.

(continued)

Table 3. (*Continued*)

Standards	Resort
Maximum density	Determination of permissible Floor Area Ratio (FAR):
	For lots less than 10,000 square feet: FAR = (.00006 × lot area) + 0.4
	For lots 10,000 square feet to 30,000 square feet: FAR = (.00002 × lot area) + 0.8
	For lots greater than 30,000 square feet: FAR = 1.4
Maximum building area	50 percent of the zoning lot
Maximum height	Maximum heights shall be as shown on the zoning maps
	Height Setbacks: For any portion of a structure over 30 feet in height, additional side and rear setbacks shall be provided; for each 10 feet of additional height or portion thereof, an additional 1 foot setback shall be provided. The additional setback shall be a continuous plane from the top of the structure to the height of 30 feet above grade.

SOURCE: Land Use Ordinance

the handful of jurisdictions requiring both county development plans and strict conformity to them by local zoning.[36] Honolulu is a good example. Eight relatively detailed land development plans, complete with maps dividing Oahu's land areas into residential (several intensity zones), commercial, industrial, public, and open space districts, set out in some detail how that land is to be used, right down to the sequence of development. A public facilities component also sets out sites for prospective transportation, solid-waste disposal, harbor, and other public facilities. The plans also locate historic, scenic, and archaeological sites.[37] After requiring the preparation and adoption of both a general plan and eight area-specific and relatively detailed development plans,[38] the Charter of the City and County of Honolulu specifically requires that "No public improvement or project, or subdivision or zoning ordinance shall be initiated or adopted unless it conforms to and implements the development plan for that area."[39] While there is room for disagreement over when nonconformity with plans that contemplate a ten-year time frame actually occurs, clearly a landowner seeking to change zoning districts so as to permit a contemplated development not allowed on the property "as zoned" must first check to see that the development plan for the area also classifies the property in a way that permits such a use. Thus, for example, developing a resort on land classified as agricultural under the applicable development plan and the LUO would require a change to the development plan map as well as an amendment to the zoning map of the LUO. The city council ultimately does both.

The development plan amendment process is likely to be the more time-consuming of the two processes (zone amendment and plan amendment) because DGP, which is responsible for the general and development plan creation (though not ultimate approval), receives and holds prospective development plan map amendments for an annual review so that all can be considered at the same time. The chief planning officer, head of DGP, "develops" proposed amendments and submits them to the planning commission for review, a public hearing, and recommendation to the city council. Then the council must hold yet another hearing before adopting (or not adopting) the amendments.[40] Thus, if a landowner were to submit a development plan amendment just after the completion of the annual review process, it would be about a year before the entire planning commission and city council proceedings could even commence. Given the hearing time and notice requirements, together with "normal" requests for extensions and delays, it is not at all unusual for the development plan amendment process alone to take two years. In part because of such delays, the DLU and DGP supported a package of city charter amendments changing the review process and substantially decreasing the level of detail in the development plans.[41] However, the new plans and new review rules were still in the drafting stage by late 1993.[42]

Rezoning and Other Changes to (and through) the LUO

After the process of development plan amendment follows the process of zoning amendment. A request for an amendment, whether to the text of the ordinance or to a zoning map, must be directed to the DLU director, in whom the charter vests authority to prepare zoning amendments. After consultation with the chief planning officer, the DLU director then refers proposed amendments to other agencies for their comment and recommendations, which must be made within forty-five days. Within ninety days of the completed application, the director then submits the proposed amendment to the planning commission, which must then hold a hearing within forty-five days and make recommendations to the city council within thirty days. The city council must then hold yet another hearing within ninety days before amending (or not amending) the LUO as proposed.[43] Once again, the process is lengthy and will easily take a year without any delays. With delays and permitted extensions (note also that there are no time limits on hearings, which can be continued indefinitely), the process can take up to three years. Like any other ordinance, a zoning ordinance must go through three readings at the council level and is generally referred to a committee (variously the zoning and planning and zoning committee over fifteen years) for recommendations to the entire council. The creation and amendment of the boundaries of the seven special districts (some of which are described more fully in Chapter 2) follow essentially the same procedure as for zoning amendments.

There are, however, a variety of other land-use changes governed by the LUO that may or may not be subject to the charter's aforementioned conformity requirement, since they are not technically amendments to the zoning ordinances, but rather conditional and special permits, reviews, and variances. They generally avoid, therefore, the lengthy development plan amendment process—but they are not necessarily expeditious.

Article 4 of the LUO specifies minimum development standards for the establishment of uses considered appropriate in some zoning districts provided certain standards and conditions are met. There are two types of these "conditional uses," labeled type 1 and type 2. The latter is the most intrusive in a particular district, for example, a foreign language school in a residential district (though it may be less intrusive—a type 1—or even permitted "of right" in other more intensive use district). As with a zoning amendment, type 2 conditional use goes to the DLU director, who submits it to other agencies for review and comment within forty-five days. The director then holds a public hearing no sooner than forty-five days from receipt of the completed application, then makes a decision within either thirty days of the end of the hearing or ninety days from the date of the completed application. A type 1 permit is simply submitted to the director, who makes a decision within ninety days.[44]

But even uses permitted "of right" are not free from administrative process. Many such uses are subject to site plan or similar review. Thus, for example, housing on sites that are "difficult to develop" under normal standards is subject to a seventy-five-day review resulting in the granting or denying of a permit to proceed. Facilities such as day care, meeting, and school facilities undergo a site plan review process that theoretically takes three months, but it must include presentation to the relevant neighborhood board and a public hearing. So-called "major projects" in any of the seven special districts undergo the same process.[45]

The last of these land-use changes is the variance, which by charter is granted by the director of the Department of Land Utilization. While theoretically an "escape valve" to permit modest development where the strict letter of the zoning ordinance would otherwise prevent it (for example, the construction of a single-family house on a 9,990 square-foot lot where the minimum lot size in the zoning district is 10,000 square feet), the variance is often misused as a substitute for necessary rezoning or special-use permits for more intensive land development.[46] The authority to hear and decide variances, originally granted to a zoning board of appeals by the Honolulu city charter,[47] is now granted to the director of DLU, who since 1984 has been granting variances anyway under a general power of "administrative reorganization" exercised by the mayor.[48] The variance request requires that there first be a public hearing where "interested persons" are afforded an opportunity to be heard. Either use (how the land is used) or bulk (set-back, side yard, front yard, height, and so forth) variances are permissible, provided that charter standards pertaining to essential character of the neighborhood, uniqueness of circumstances, and hardship on the applicant are met.[49]

County Land-Use Permits Outside Zoning Ordinances:
Coastal Zone and Floodplain

Counties in Hawaii also issue permits for coastal area developments, made necessary by county ordinances passed pursuant to state and federal coastal and floodplain protection laws. The most prominent—but not necessarily the most stringent—of these is the shoreline management permit (SMP, or SMA permit), issued pursuant to coastal zone management statutes at the state and federal level.

The federal coastal zone management act, or FCZMA, offers funds for the creation and administration of a state coastal zone management and regulation program to all states who will follow selected federal guidelines, described in greater detail in Chapter 6. This substantial federal funding, together with the review of federal projects on federal lands (otherwise exempt from state and local regulatory activity) that a "consistency" (with a federally approved coastal zone management program) review provides, persuaded Hawaii to join the program in 1978. Among the three alternatives for controlling and managing the coastal zone, Hawaii chose one that grants its four counties effective regulatory control over proposed developments in the landward area of the zone.

Basically, no development may proceed in a shoreline management area (SMA) without an SMP. Aside from routine maintenance of shoreline and roadways, development includes virtually everything from building a house to developing a resort hotel. The so-called "regulatory" coastal zone extends virtually unbroken around each of Hawaii's islands, and for a considerable distance inland to include coastal floodplains, unique environments and habitats, and recreational areas.[50] Hawaii's courts have upheld expansive interpretations of this regulatory coastal zone while sharply curtailing the authority of the counties to deny SMPs without close linkage to permit standards.[51] In the counties other than Honolulu, such permits are administered by the county's planning commissions. In Honolulu, however, SMPs are administered by the city council, producing not only inconsistency among the counties, but an odd court case that leaves only Honolulu's SMPs out of the reach of the state's Administrative Procedures Act.[52]

In Honolulu, DLU first receives an application, and after compliance with HEIS (discussed earlier in this chapter)—since a development within an SMA is de facto a development triggering the need for an environmental assessment—DLU holds a public hearing within twenty to sixty days. It must then make a recommendation to the city council within ten days of the close of the hearing. The council then has sixty days to grant or deny the SMP.[53] In the event that HEIS produces an assessment but no EIS, the DLU director may require an EIS whenever he determines that a proposed development may significantly affect an SMA and that sufficient information to evaluate those effects is unavailable.[54]

The federal government also provides money for the administration of a flood insurance program, dependent upon intense state and local regulation of flood-prone areas. As in many other states, Hawaii chooses to regulate these flood-prone areas at the county level, largely through county subdivision ordinances.

The federal government issued guidelines for the regulation of so-called 100-year floodplains (more fully described in Chapter 6) for the purpose of limiting development in areas where it provides disaster protection relief. Basically, the federal government will not provide such relief to states that have not enacted such development regulations, nor will it permit federally insured lending institutions to make mortgage loans in flood-prone areas where no such regulatory system is in effect. The regulations must provide for a series of surveys and maps, each step resulting in a progressively more stringent set of land development regulations in the regulatory (100-year) floodplain, until finally virtually no development is permitted unless the lowest habitable floor is located one foot above the highest wash of the likely water level in the event of a 100-year flood.

Hawaii is a participating state, and its counties promulgate and administer floodplain regulations through subdivision codes, more fully discussed in the next section. Basically, each development must comply with the federally sponsored guidelines prohibiting development in the floodplain, briefly described above. Variances are permitted, but for Hawaii to remain in the program, these variances must be in accordance with strict standards, again federally-mandated.

Subdivision and Land Development

Even after all land-use permissions are granted, most land developers find themselves faced with the requirements of a development code of some sort, particularly if the contemplated land use is a residential development. This triggers the requirements of the state subdivision statute and its implementation under the subdivision ordinances of the respective counties. Again, Honolulu provides a good example. While the subdivision ordinance (and any amendments) is ultimately passed by the city council, it is initially prepared by the DLU director and reviewed (public hearing, findings, and recommendations) by the planning commission. Review of subdivisions themselves, however, as well as the promulgation of rules and regulations governing such an approach, are up to the director. The rules prohibit the subdividing of land, the selling of any interest in land located in a subdivision (that is, a lot), or the recording of a plat of subdivision unless a final plan has been approved by the director. New state law allows advertising and reservation prior to the final plan if the subdivision is registered with the state. Moreover, no roadway may be opened or any building occupied until the director approves the public improvements required by the rules and regulations. Appeals of the director's decisions are heard by the zoning board of appeals. In Hawaii County, no building permit will be issued until after approval and acceptance of roads, which further delays construction of residential units.

Honolulu follows a traditional two-step process in the review of subdivisions. An applicant files fifteen copies of a preliminary map with the DLU director. Among the requirements for the preliminary map are the detailed location and dimensions of each lot, location and dimension of existing and proposed streets, slope and contour lines, locations of landmarks and flood/inundation zones, proposed use (residence, park, public building, and so forth) of each lot, and existing and proposed infrastructure (sewer, water, landscaping).

Copies of the map are distributed to other county and state agencies for review and comment at the same time DLU conducts its own review. The director has very little discretion in preliminary map approval. Tentative approval means that the preliminary map conforms with the rules and regulations promulgated, and the applicant may submit a detailed plan, provided the developer dedicates land for things such as streets and parks (roads, streets, drainage, sewers, water, landscaping) and constructs or guarantees construction (by performance bond) of certain improvements, to assure they are in fact completed. Next, subdivision construction plans and permits are prepared and reviewed, a process that typically takes a year or more. The final map must conform to the approved preliminary map. The decision of the director on this point is purely ministerial, the sole question being whether or not the preliminary map conforms.

Conclusion

The foregoing represents a cut at the major land-use changes and permits necessary to undertake any but the most insignificant land development in Hawaii. Between state and local requirements, seven to eight years would appear to be an almost reasonable amount of time for the completion of a project from the day the first application is filed. Individually, each permit and land-use change described above has merit. Collectively, the regulatory maze is overwhelming. Is all this process necessary? More important, is it *due* process, or are we temporarily *taking* property without due process of law?

Thus, for example, our golf course resort development (from Chapter 1) would need a variety of permits and reclassification unless, in the unlikely event the land was in the urban district (unlikely because unless it were in the reserve for future development, such large acreages are not usually found in the urban district). LUC records indicate that such proposed uses are located primarily on land classified in the state agricultural district instead. The property would need to be either wholly reclassified into the urban district or partly so classified (for the resort buildings), with the rest the subject of combined state-county permits in the agricultural district for whatever part of the golf course is on "prime" land, potentially "of right" (no need for further state permits) if on "poor" land. There is some dispute over whether further county zoning is necessary in the latter event. If any of the property is in the coastal zone, at least an environmental assessment if not a full-blown EIS would be necessary under HEIS. Water-quality permits might also be required.

At the county level in Honolulu, a development plan map amendment would also be necessary, through the present annual review process. After that (sometimes concurrently) a zoning map amendment would also be necessary, with the possibility of special- or conditional-use permits required. The coastal nature of the property and location of the proposed resort buildings in the coastal zone would also require an SMA permit under the county implementation of the coastal zone management act. In the event such structures are also in a tsunami inundation zone, as mapped under county administration of the federal Disaster Protection Act, compliance with those portions of the county subdivision ordinances would also be necessary. Of course, a dredge and fill permit from the Corps of Engineers under Section 404 of the federal Clean Water Act would almost certainly be necessary as well.

The foregoing does not deal with other potential permits, of which Honolulu alone lists just under one hundred in its published permit register. These are *not* the "normal delays in obtaining building permits, changes in zoning ordinances, variances and the like" that Chief Justice Rehnquist of the U.S. Supreme Court had in mind in 1987, and that would likely be immune from regulatory takings challenges.

Regulating for Environmental Protection: Coastal Protection, Wetlands, and Clean Air and Water

The protection of the physical environment has proceeded with great vigor at the federal, state, and local government levels in the United States since at least the early 1970s.[1] Hawaii is no exception. There are regulatory programs to protect the coastal zone, preserve wetlands, and provide for clean air and water. All of the above programs are either mandated or encouraged (by means of federal funds, usually) at the federal level, to be administered either by the State of Hawaii or the four counties. All of these programs have worthwhile environmental purposes and all protect parts of our island environment that most of us agree are worth preserving. However, to the extent that environmental regulations prevent economic use of land by a private landowner while protecting something less than the *human* environment for health and safety, they may well constitute a regulatory taking for which compensation must be paid. At least since the 1992 decision of the U.S. Supreme Court in *Lucas* (see Chapter 1), regulations protecting only the public welfare are at serious legal risk.

The Legal Context

The protection of the environment through the use of police power regulations is hardly new, but the increasingly explicit language of the U.S. Supreme Court when dealing with regulations designed to protect the environment in a land-use context is. Thus, for example, we have the Court in *Keystone Bituminous Coal v. Debenedictis*[2] declaring (in a 5 to 4 opinion) that if a regulation promotes the health, *environment*, or fiscal integrity of the people, it not only meets the test for sufficient state interest, but may virtually eliminate as well all economic use of private land to which it is applied. The court suggested in another decision the same year that although the line between environmental and land-use planning "will not always be bright . . . . [T]he core activity described by each phrase is undoubtedly different. Land use planning in essence chooses particular uses for the land; environmental regulation, at its core, does not mandate particular uses of the land but requires only that, however the land is used, damage to the environment is kept within prescribed limits."[3]

In both instances, however, the question is whether the Court had in mind just the human environment or—if separable—the natural environment apart from the human environment as well. Clear examples of the latter would be regulations protecting endangered species, the destruction of which poses little known threat to humans.[4] Less clear perhaps are regulations designed to protect, say, wetlands. This may well be an important distinction if one is to judge from the transcript of oral argument in the *Lucas* case:

> *Scalia*: The South Carolina court analogizes to wetlands regulation. They don't think they have to look at economic use. *I don't think wetlands regulation is something that I would call one of the high concerns of public safety.*[5]

The clear implication of Justice Scalia's remarks is that the economic effect of such as wetlands regulations will be examined far more carefully than, say, a pure public health or safety regulation such as building heights or prohibiting industrial uses in residential zones. After reading the majority opinion Justice Scalia wrote in *Lucas*, it is equally clear that the majority of the Court shares some of these views about the relatively lesser importance of environmental regulations.

Justice Scalia is particularly concerned with regulations that deprive the owner of substantially all economically beneficial use "for the common good," as distinguished from those regulations that aim to protect the public from nuisance-like uses with health and safety implications. He says, for example, that "affirmatively supporting a compensation requirement is the fact that regulations that leave the owner of land without economically beneficial or productive options for its use—*typically, as here, by requiring land to be left in its natural state*—carry with them a heightened risk that private property is being pressed into some form of public service under the guise of mitigating *serious public harm.*" The implication is clear: serious public harm might conceivably support leaving land in its natural state for such as coastal flood hazard protection purposes, but "public service" does not. The majority opinion continues a few paragraphs later in the same vein:

> The many statutes on the books, both state and federal, that provide for the use of eminent domain to impose servitudes on private scenic lands preventing developmental uses, or to acquire such lands altogether, suggest the practical equivalence in this setting of negative regulation and appropriation.
>
> * * *
>
> We think, in short, that there are good reasons for our frequently expressed belief that when the owner of real property has been called upon to sacrifice *all* economically beneficial uses *in the name of the common good*, that is, to leave his property economically idle, he has suffered a taking.

The Court then emphasizes over and over the factual allegations that the South Carolina beachfront protection law was meant to protect "an extremely valuable public resource." The Court continues:

> It is quite possible, for example, to describe in *either* fashion the ecological, economic, and aesthetic concerns that inspired the South Carolina legislature in the present case. One could say that imposing a servitude on Lucas's land is necessary in order to prevent his use of it from "harming" South Carolina's ecological resources; or, instead, in order to achieve the "benefits" of an ecological preserve.
>
> * * *
>
> Whether Lucas's construction of single-family residences on his parcels should be described as bringing "harm" to South Carolina's adjacent

ecological resources thus depends principally upon whether the descri-
ber believes that the State's use interest in nurturing those resources is
as important that *any* competing adjacent use must yield.

Nor will the mere *recitation* of harmful, nuisance-like activity save
a regulation: "We emphasize that to win its case South Carolina
must do more than proffer the legislature's declaration that the uses
Lucas desires are inconsistent with the public interest or the con-
clusory assertion that they violate a common law maxim such as
sic utere . . . ." [the Latin phrase which is the basis for the exercise
of the police power in the land use context]." As the Court's majority further noted, the test for requiring compensation cannot be
"whether the legislature has recited a harm-preventing justification
for its action. . . . Since such a justification can be formulated in
practically every case, this amounts to a test of whether the legislature has a stupid staff. We think the Takings Clause requires courts
to do more than insist upon artful harm-preventing characterizations."

As with historic preservation and aesthetic regulations discussed
in Chapter 4, courts will require compensation for environmental
regulations such as those for wetland protection that devalue private property more readily than for human health and safety. To
preserve such regulations, it will be necessary to forge strong links
to public (human) health. Indeed, this is a major issue in the *Lucas*
case, where the state shoreline protection legislation seeks primarily to protect coastal resources (views, endangered species, and so
forth) but also to protect property and life from such as flood
damage—always assuming these are not the recitations of "a
harm-preventing justification for its action," which the *Lucas*
court has castigated as "artful harm-preventing characterizations."

Coastal Protection: Not a "High Concern of Public Safety"?

For nearly twenty years, the federal government has fostered coastal zone management and protection through FCZMA. Designed
largely to encourage states in coastal areas to plan, manage, and
regulate the use of land therein, the FCZMA provides funds for the
creation and implementation of a state coastal zone management

plan on the condition that the state follows federal coastal zone land management and regulatory guidelines. In the 1970s Hawaii responded to this federal coastal zone management and protection initiative with a state coastal zone management act that divided coastal zone management and protection between the state and the four counties.[6]

Administered at the state level by OSP, through its Coastal Zone Management Plan (CZMP) division, actual land development permitting takes place at the county level, as discussed in Chapter 5. Essentially, the four counties grant SMPs for virtually any meaningful development in the so-called "regulatory" coastal zone. This zone varies from two hundred yards to over a mile in width, in order to control shorelines, the use of which has a direct and significant impact on coastal waters.[7] Hawaii's courts appear so far to uphold a fairly wide regulatory zone drawn by the counties, coupled, however, with a warning that counties cannot deny SMA permits without clear and strong evidence that proposed uses will adversely affect coastal zone values.[8] These standards for administering the coastal zone management (CZM) program generally, coupled with the standards for issuing (or not issuing) SMA permits, put the program at risk after *Lucas*. The emphasis is almost entirely on welfare rather than human health and safety.

First, the general standards guiding the program: in implementing the objectives of the CZM program, the agencies "shall give full consideration to ecological, cultural, historic, aesthetic, recreational, scenic, and open space values, and coastal hazards, as well as to needs for economic development."[9] These statutory objectives and policies are binding on all the agencies dealing with the coastal zone. Only the single objective or policy category of coastal hazards deals with health and safety.

Second, the SMA permit process: a permit is required whenever development as defined by the Hawaii Coastal Zone Management Act (HCZMA) occurs. About the only development not needing a permit is a single-family house not part of a larger project. Although the HCZMA provides for three types of permits, only the SMP affects land value in a meaningful way. Such a permit authorizes development with a value in excess of $125,000, or which may have a substantial adverse environmental or ecological effect.[10] The statutory guidelines for county agencies in deciding whether or not to grant an SMP refine what environmental or ecological effect means. All the guidelines are directed at managing the coastal zone with a conservation/preservation goal. Certainly those guidelines directed at protecting human health and safety (such as those ensuring that any construction and "alterations to existing land forms and vegetation" cause minimal danger of floods, landslides, erosion, siltation, or failure in the event of earthquake, or adversely affect water quality) would pass constitutional muster. Indeed, most of these border on nuisance abatement that even the most conservative of the nine justices of the USSCT would find acceptable regulations under the police power regardless of the economic effect on private property.

Other SMA statutory guidelines, however, are not so clearly related to human health and safety. Reasonable terms and conditions set by the permitting authority are also designed to ensure that land alterations and construction cause minimum adverse effect to scenic and recreational amenities; ensure adequate access, by dedication or other means, to publicly owned or used beaches, recreation areas, and natural reserves; and ensure that adequate and properly located public recreation areas and wildlife preserves are reserved.[11] Development to be minimized: that which would reduce the size of any beach or reduce other area usable for public recreation; impose restrictions upon public access to tidal and submerged lands, beaches, and portions of rivers and streams within the SMA; or substantially interfere with or detract from the line of sight toward the sea from the state highway nearest the coast; or adversely affect existing areas of open water free of visible structures, wildlife habitats, or potential or existing agricultural uses of land.[12]

These concerns, however important and laudable, are at best welfare concerns, some of which are only marginally related even to the coastal zone. Under recent state court modifications of regulatory taking criteria (such as the decision by the California appeals court in *First Lutheran Church*, discussed in Chapter 1, which the U.S. Supreme Court, given an opportunity to modify, let stand), such regulations at the very least will be subject to heightened scrutiny with respect to the economic damage they cause private property. Under *Lucas*, (which deals with a state statute that also mixes some human health and safety with a lot of welfare), regulations based upon such standards and criteria are also likely to fail constitutionally if they deprive a landowner of economically beneficial use or leave only very little of the same. The *Lucas* court is quite clear about its disdain for conferring public benefit at the expense of a private landowner.

Wetlands

Giving wetlands preservation priority over all or most economic use becomes even less defensible without clearly relating that preservation to human health and safety. As the quotation from Justice Scalia and the analysis of *Lucas* above clearly demonstrate, wetland protection is likely to fall squarely into the welfare box rather than the health and safety box.

Recall from Chapter 5 that the Army Corps of Engineers requires a permit under Section 404 of the Clean Water Act for any proposed discharge of dredge or fill material into the waters of the United States.[13] A district engineer usually makes the determination of whether a permit should be granted or not. Recall also that it is very difficult to undertake development in a coastal zone without depositing material in a U.S. waterway. Moreover, it is altogether impossible to develop any wetland area without depositing dredge or fill material.

The factors the district engineer must consider in an application for a Section 404 permit include a "public interest review," which is essentially a broad balancing of economic and environmental factors on a case-by-case basis.[14] Weighing "benefits which may be expected to accrue" from a proposed activity against its "reasonably foreseeable detriments," the district engineer considers the following factors:

> conservation, economics, aesthetics, general environmental concerns, wetlands, historic properties, fish and wildlife values, *flood hazards, floodplain values,* land use, *navigation, shore erosion and accretion,* recreation, *water supply and conservation, water quality, energy needs,*

safety, food and fiber production, mineral needs, considerations of property ownership, and, in general, the needs and welfare of the people.[15]

The public interest review guidelines for the Corps do not allow the granting of a dredge and fill permit for a wetland that serves an important public function unless the benefits of altering the wetland outweigh damage to the wetland. The specific public functions that wetlands serve and that the Corps guidelines declare to be "important" include:

(i) Wetlands which serve significant natural biological functions, including food chain production, general habitat and nesting, spawning, rearing, and resting sites for aquatic or land species;

(ii) Wetlands set aside for study of the aquatic environment or as sanctuaries or refuges;

(iii) Wetlands the destruction or alteration of which would affect detrimentally the natural drainage characteristics, sedimentation patterns, salinity distribution, flushing characteristics, current patterns, or other environmental characteristics;

(iv) *Wetlands which are significant in shielding other areas from wave action, erosion, or storm damage. Such wetlands are often associated with barrier beaches, islands, reefs and bars;*

(v) *Wetlands which serve as valuable storage areas for storm and flood waters;*

(vi) *Wetlands which are ground water discharge areas that maintain minimum baseflows important to aquatic resources and those which are prime natural recharge areas;*

(vii) *Wetlands which serve significant water purification functions;*

(viii) Wetlands which are unique in nature or scarce in quantity to the region or local area.[16]

The same regulations also require that the district engineer consider the effect of a project on values, such as projects associated with:

wild and scenic rivers, historic properties and National Landmarks, National Rivers, National Wilderness Areas, National Seashores, National Recreation Areas, National Lakeshores, National Parks, National Monuments, estuarine and marine sanctuaries, archeological resources, including Indian religious or cultural sites, and such other areas as may be established under federal or state laws for similar and related purposes.[17]

Aside from the italicized values and criteria, the standards are exclusively welfare, rather than health and safety, in nature. Even before *Lucas*, some federal courts sharply curbed the Corps' authority in both the designation and protection of wetlands.[18] No wonder Justice Scalia could not find much of a public health and safety rationale for preserving wetlands! Important as they otherwise may be, justifying the failure to grant a permit for dredge and fill on private property that substantially deprives the owner of economic use of the land will be difficult.

Flood Hazards

In stark contrast to coastal zone regulations, the purpose for local regulation of flood hazard areas is to protect public health, safety, and property. It is for this purpose that the federal Disaster Protection Act sets out standards that, if adopted locally, forbid most construction in coastal high hazard and 100-year floodplain lands. The act itself does not prevent such construction because, like the FCZMA, the federal government provides money to state and local governments, along with other inducements, in order to persuade them to enact floodplain regulations. This is the situation in Hawaii, where all four counties have passed appropriate floodplain regulations and are, accordingly, participating in the federal flood hazard program.[19]

Honolulu's flood hazard district (7.10 of the Land Use Ordinance) is typical both in terms of articulated purpose and severe restriction of land use in the most hazardous of the flood districts:

Certain areas within the City are subject to periodic inundation by flooding and/or tsunami which may result in the loss of life and property, creation of health and safety hazards, disruption of commerce and governmental services as well as extraordinary public expenditures for flood and tsunami protection and relief. The purposes of establishing

Flood Hazard Districts are to protect life and property and reduce public costs for flood control and rescue and relief efforts, thereby promoting the safety, health, convenience and general welfare of the community.

After stating that the entire flood hazard zone section is passed because of the federal Flood Disaster Protection Act, the section proceeds to divide flood hazard districts into four (floodway, flood fringe, coastal high hazard, and general flood plain), as delineated on Flood Insurance Rate Maps (FIRMs), prepared by the Federal Emergency Management Agency of the Federal Insurance Administration. As would be expected, the toughest land-use controls apply to the floodway district, where flood waters are most likely to pass most frequently and with the greatest velocity:

Within the Floodway District, the following uses having a low flood damage potential and not obstructing the regulatory flood shall be permitted as under the underlying zoning district and which are not prohibited by any other laws or ordinances; and provided they do not affect the capacity of the floodway or any tributary or any other drainage facility or system:

1. Public and private outdoor recreational facilities, lawn, garden and play areas.

2. Agricultural uses including farming, grazing, pasture and outdoor plant nurseries.

3. Drainage improvements, such as dams, levees, channels and bridges.

Temporary or permanent structures, fill, storage of material or equipment or other improvements which affect the capacity of the floodway or increase the regulatory flood elevations shall not be allowed. Construction and improvements shall be subject to documentation by studies and data by a registered professional engineer that, to the best available technical knowledge and information, encroachment shall not result in any increase in the regulatory flood elevations during occurrence of the regulatory flood [usually defined as one which occurs every 100 years].[20]

In the coastal high hazard district, all construction and improvements must have the lowest floor, including basements, elevated to or above the regulatory flood elevation and "securely anchored" to piles and columns to resist movement and flotation.[21]

It is difficult to imagine much more stringent regulation of development, at least in the regulatory flood zone, which prohibits virtually all structural use. Coastal high hazard is not much better, given the expansive elevation requirements. However, the health and safety justifications for the regulations would appear to be overwhelming. It is thus difficult to see how these regulations would be vulnerable under any but the most libertarian interpretation of the takings clause.[22]

Clean Air

Hawaii's Department of Health (DOH) has promulgated a series of regulations requiring a permit from the director of the department for most major construction activity, in order to control air pollution. The basis for this regulation is the federal Clean Air Act, provisions of which are directed squarely at land development—principally by means of stationary source controls—and in which states and local governments have no choice but to comply. Basically, the Clean Air Act provides for geographically uniform federal quality standards for ambient air (the air around us) to be established for pollutants named by the administrator of the EPA. These standards are enforced at the state level by means of State Implementation Plans, or SIPs. The Clean Air Act also provides for the promulgation of emission standards (for air at a point of discharge into the atmosphere) for new "stationary sources" of pollution (factories, power plants, and so forth), for certain hazardous pollutants, and for pollutants from motor vehicles.[23]

While Hawaii has relatively few stationary sources emitting the kinds of pollutants that fall under the Clean Air Act, DOH has set out standards for new stationary sources. Basically, no one may conduct any activity that causes air pollution without written approval of the director of DOH. Such an activity includes, obviously, a new stationary source of pollution. A stationary source is any property that emits or may emit any air pollutant. Indeed, with respect to new sources, no one may even construct anything that might emit air pollutants without the director's authority. Moreover, authority to construct such a stationary source does not mean the director will issue a necessary permit to operate the source, once constructed.[24] There are exceptions, but they are insignificant. The question is, therefore, what are the conditions for permits and permissions?

Basically, the director "shall" approve construction if best available control technology (BACT) is provided to control the pollutants the EPA has identified and for which it has set (or the state has set) ambient air quality standards. If the source is a major one, it must also meet standards designed to prevent significant deterioration (PSD) of air quality. An exception can be made for facilities to be constructed in the public interest, according to state statutes. A variety of other requirements having to do with phasing of larger projects and the like may apply as well, depending upon the nature of the new stationary source.[25]

Essentially, then, DOH will need to approve most new nonresidential construction in Hawaii and perhaps even large multifamily projects that use incineration as a waste disposal method. While this can have significant effects on the land development process, it is unlikely that imposing these regulations will actually stop or seriously affect the economics of a proposed land development. Therefore, the likelihood is remote that sufficient economic damage could be done so as to give rise to a regulatory taking of property claim. Moreover, the public health rationale for imposing Clean Air Act guidelines are sufficiently substantial that such regulations would probably pass constitutional muster even if the economic burden on private property were substantial.[26]

Clean Water

The federal Clean Water Act has as its principal purpose the cleaning and maintenance of the nation's waters. It does so by means of both "structural" (funds for such as publicly owned wastewater treatment works, or POTWs) and "nonstructural" (regulatory) means. The purpose of both is to eliminate discharge of pollutants in the nation's waterways, both coastal and continental. Inherent in both methodologies is implementation by state and local government.[27] For purposes of this book, the issue is the purpose behind the regulatory aspect of the Hawaii program that most affects land development: NPDES as administered by DOH, in accordance with federally mandated water quality standards.

As with the Clean Air Act, the EPA (this time in conjunction with each state) establishes standards for pollutant discharges into waterways. By far the most important of these, particularly for Hawaii, are effluent standards, which apply to named pollutants being discharged from a particular or "point" (as opposed to run-off) source. The enforcement of these standards is controlled by the section of the Clean Water Act forbidding the discharge of any pollutant into a waterway without a permit. This is the heart of the NPDES system. In 1974, Hawaii was granted authority by the EPA to issue NPDES permits for all discharges except those from a federal facility. While the primary discharge permits are for sources such as steam electrical generating plants and sugar mills, essentially any discharger is covered by an NPDES permit administered by the health department.[28] More pollution, in fact, comes from nonpoint sources of pollution, for which the state has not yet adopted standards (agricultural, silvicultural, and construction run-off, for example). Until such standards are adopted, these activities are not regulated.

As compared with the Clean Air Act, however, the articulated policy of the State of Hawaii regarding clean water is heavily tinged with welfare, as opposed to health and safety, purposes. This may make the policy more vulnerable to challenge, to the extent that NPDES permit conditions or outright denial substantially reduce the value of private property. The state's policy is:

1. To conserve the waters of the State;
2. To protect, maintain and improve the quality thereof:

    A. For drinking water supply, and food processing;

    B. For the growth, support and propagation of shellfish, fish and other desirable species of marine and aquatic life;

    C. For oceanographic research;

    D. For the conservation of coral reefs and wilderness areas;

E. For domestic, agricultural, industrial, other legitimate uses;

3. To provide that no waste be discharged into any waters of this state without first being given the degree of treatment necessary to protect the legitimate beneficial uses of such waters;

4. To provide for the prevention, abatement, and control of new and existing water pollution;

5. To cooperate with the federal government in carrying out these objectives[.][29]

DOH rules then require an application for an NPDES permit from any person discharging any pollutant (or substantially increasing or altering the quality of any discharge) into a waterway, and sets out detailed application procedures and requirements.[30]

Most critical in the decision of whether or not to issue an NPDES permit is compliance with effluent standards (though standards of performance for new sources also apply). For this purpose, DOH divides the waters of Hawaii into several classes, with different objectives and standards applied to each. Thus, for example, the uses to be protected in "Class 1.a." waters are "scientific and educational purposes, protection of breeding stock and baseline references from which human-caused changes can be measured, compatible recreation, aesthetic enjoyment, and other nondegrading uses which are compatible with the protection of the ecosystems associated with waters of this class."[31] Recreation and aesthetic enjoyment are listed as purposes in most of the classifications.

These are, of course, hardly invalid concerns. The problem is, once again, that many of them relate to public welfare rather than public health and safety. It is easy to envision the difficulty in obtaining NPDES permits for land-based activities requiring discharge of pollutants into waterways. Clearly, many of the reasons for not granting such permits will have less to do with public health and safety and more to do with protecting aesthetic and recreational values. To this extent they are vulnerable, given the current direction of regulatory takings law at the federal level, particularly after the *Lucas* case.

Environmental regulations, particularly those enforced at the state and local governmental levels, generally are squarely impacted by the regulatory takings standards after *Lucas*. Particularly vulnerable are coastal zone management regulations, the SMA permit process, and certain aspects of the NPDES process under the Clean Water Act.

CHAPTER 7

Conclusion: Alternatives to Regulation for Protecting the Public Welfare

The foregoing chapters paint a rather bleak picture for the preservation of open space, wetlands, coastal resources, parts of the built environment, and exactions and fees for such as low-income housing through the regulation of land. However, there are alternatives. This chapter discusses the use of private organizations such as the Nature Conservancy and PATH, private devices such as restrictive covenants and servitudes, and the public trust doctrine as reasonable alternatives to using police power to preserve these land-use values and produce necessary housing. The chapter also discusses new legislative solutions to due process problems caused by inordinate delay in the land-use development approval process.

Open Space, Coastal Resource, and Other Natural Features Preservation Through Purchase: The Nature Conservancy

One of the surest ways to preserve natural features in this or any other state is to buy them. Since government funds are limited, this often means substantial support from the private sector. In Hawaii, such support has been forthcoming mainly from Hawaii's Nature Conservancy.

Established in 1980 as a nonprofit organization and part of the forty-year-old international Nature Conservancy, the Nature Conservancy of Hawaii has helped to protect more than 48,000 acres of natural areas through a variety of techniques. Among these are the establishment and inventorying of a data base of areas needing protection in Hawaii, the drafting of cooperative management agreements between government and private landowners for natural areas protection, and public education through sponsored expeditions, tours, publications, and workshops.

But the Nature Conservancy's most effective technique is the purchase and management or transfer, with strict preservation conditions, of large parcels of land. For example, the Conservancy and the State of Hawaii jointly purchased and transferred the 11,000-acre Kipahulu Valley in Maui to Haleakala National Park. Conservancy interests on the slopes of Mauna Kea on the island of Hawaii were also transferred for management purposes to FWS as part of the Hakalau Refuge, estimated to eventually grow to 31,000 acres. In addition, the Conservancy owns and manages ten preserves on five Hawaiian islands, ranging in size from the thirty-acre Ihiihilauakea Preserve in a shallow crater on Oahu's southeast coast above Hanauma Bay, to the 5,759-acre Pelekunu Preserve on Molokai's north coast.

Development Rights Transfer: A Public Alternative

The private sector will not always be able to step in to purchase resource areas that the public would like to see preserved. Therefore, it is useful to consider the acquisition and transfer of development rights to such resource areas by government either as an alternative or addition to such private acquisition.

The transfer of development rights (TDR) from one parcel to another is an increasingly common technique to preserve both historic structures and open space.[1] It has even been sanctioned by the U.S. Supreme Court for the preservation of historic buildings.[2] Moreover, Honolulu already uses the technique to permit private developers to build taller buildings than might otherwise be permitted by acquiring air rights from nearby lots and transferring them to the development lot.[3] Essentially, the technique permits the transfer of air rights from parcel A to parcel B in order to compensate the owner of parcel A for otherwise permissible development that the public deems inappropriate but that may not be regulated away, particularly after the *Lucas* decision. The key is the severability of development rights from the land. The rights are either purchased by another landowner in order to increase the allowable height and density on his or her parcel, used by the landowner of both parcels to increase the density and height on one while leaving the density and height "as is" on the other, or purchased by government so as to permanently decrease the density or use of land on the parcel from which the rights are acquired. In each case, a particular parcel becomes more or less free of development, thus preserving a building, a coastline, a landmark, a cultural site—all of which are more difficult to preserve by regulation after *Lucas*.

However, relying on the private sector alone to purchase the development rights for use or transfer elsewhere also raises taking-issue problems, unless the government is at least available as a backup purchaser. This is so because if there is no instant market for such rights, then when a landowner wants to develop, for example, a significant coastal area, mountaintop, or historic site, there is no compensation for the loss of development rights because no one is available to purchase them. This has led some commentators to suggest that if valuable wetlands, beaches, open spaces, agricultural lands, and so forth, are to be preserved after *Lucas*, a public development rights bank needs to be established to at least make a market for, if not purchase in the first instance, such severed development rights. These rights would then be sold in areas where higher density development is contemplated, thereby replenishing the fund, at least in part. Otherwise, the property owner bears the brunt of resource protection economically, vastly increasing the likelihood that a court will find a taking by regulation after *Lucas*. According to one commentator, such a TDR program would work like this:

1. State or county funds, most probably from a bond issue so designated, would be divided into several revolving funds, each containing twenty to thirty million dollars.
2. Administration of each fund would depend upon its purpose. A historic preservation fund might be jointly administered by

DLNR and Historic Hawaii Foundation. A coastal resources protection fund might be jointly administered by OSP and DLNR, and so forth.

3. Areas to be preserved and areas where transferred rights could be used for development would be identified, perhaps on either existing functional or development plans. If non-resource development areas are not identified, then the funds will soon be depleted. Preservation areas from which rights would be purchased for holding and eventual transfer might include beaches, wetlands, wildlife habitats, plant habitats, prime agricultural land, mountain areas, and historic/cultural sites.

4. Clear administrative mechanisms would be drawn up to ensure that landowners in areas to be protected would quickly and easily be able to sell the development rights to their property if they so chose.[4]

Housing: Public Programs and Private "PATHs"

The use of set-asides and other police power mechanisms for the production of low-income housing has not been particularly successful in Hawaii for a variety of reasons discussed in Chapter 4. Estimates are that the State of Hawaii will need 64,000 additional units of affordable housing by the year 2000.[5] Not only is it difficult to envision the construction of "at market" housing to enable a set-aside percentage of low-income housing of any signficance, but the use of such set-asides presumes a strong, if not booming, residential construction market. But Hawaii has not consistently maintained such a market. Therefore, significant gains are likely only through the funding of substantial amounts of low-income housing from government or quasi government sources.

The first source of major significance in Hawaii is HFDC. Carved out of HHA in the late 1980s largely to build affordable housing, this state development corporation constructed 2,100 homes by the end of 1991, with 5,000 more "on the drawing board." As noted in Chapter 4, HFDC has firm plans for at least 13,000 of these units at three principal sites on three islands: 4,200 in west Hawaii, 4,300 on Maui, and the rest in eight villages on Oahu, primarily in the new community of Kapolei in Ewa. While the emphasis has so far been on the relatively expensive single-family detached homes, future developments are expected to provide a mix of multifamily units as well, though primarily for sale rather than for rent. If it meets its goals, HFDC will account for a substantial reduction of the large deficit in Hawaii's affordable housing stock.

A second source of major signficance is PATH, the proposed Hawaii Nonprofit Housing Development Corporation. Founded in 1992 as a response to government requests for affordable housing increments along the proposed Honolulu fixed-rail transit system, the corporation is a joint venture of the prime developer of the system and The Myers Corporation. Managed by a board of private and public sector representatives, PATH expects to use several million dollars in public and private grants and contributions to develop at least 5,000 affordable rental units in existing and projected urban neighborhoods along transit corridors in Honolulu over the next ten years. Modeled after San Francisco's successful Bridge Housing Corporation, PATH is a Section 501(c)(3) public benefit nonprofit corporation. It has the capacity to

—create new affordable housing as well as acquire, improve, and preserve existing affordable housing;
—link public and private sources of debt and equity financing for affordable housing;
—bring new resources, such as Hawaii Community Reinvestment Corporation financing and private equity, to the table to address local affordable housing needs;
—collaborate with existing affordable housing organizations to enhance the affordable housing development capacity in the county.

The September 1992 vote of the city council to rescind support for Honolulu's proposed fixed-guideway rapid transit system has substantially decreased the ability to place such housing along a fixed-transit corridor and resulted in the withdrawal of one million dollars in private funds from the consortium that had expected to

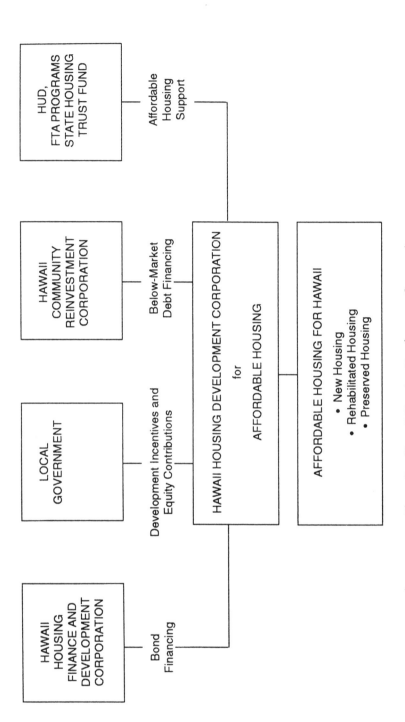

Figure 2. Hawaii Housing Development Corporation

construct the system. Nevertheless, PATH remains committed to constructing the 5,000 units.

The "Public Trust" for Coastal Conservation

Well established in American jurisprudence is the principle that bottomlands and tidelands under and along navigable waterways may be used privately, if at all, subject to a public "estate in land" that cannot be extinguished, even by a state itself. Rooted in sixth-century Roman law, this public-trust concept is accepted judicially in nearly forty states, including Hawaii. Basically, the doctrine prohibits the state from allowing or making use of public trust lands (more precisely, the public legal interest or, in legalese, the "estate" in these lands) in a way that adversely affects the rights of the public to those lands.

While the public trust doctrine has traditionally applied only to bottomlands (submerged lands) and tidelands (to the upper reach of the waves), it has often included dry sand beaches.[6] Gradually, the idea that activities affecting adjacent public trust-encumbered lands might also be regulated has taken root. Courts have, for example, on more than one occasion supported the federal government's regulation of adjacent private land to protect federal land resources. Other state supreme courts have considerably expanded the notion of public trust protection over activities that might affect public trust titles.[7]

Hawaii courts have also applied the concept of public trust to give the State of Hawaii title to eight acres of newly created shoreland resulting from volcanic activity on the island of Hawaii.[8] Courts have held that private uses interfering with access, fishing, and similar activities to be interferences with the public rights in public trust (submerged and tidal) lands.[9] Private docks and water pollution with the potential for diminishing fish have been held to violate the public trust doctrine.

Partly based on these experiences, some have suggested that coastal zone resources traditionally protected by the exercise of state police power can as easily be rested on the public trust doctrine.[10] Thus, for example, marina and other waterfront development can be made to conform to local concepts of public trust use of bottom and tidelands. Acting as a "property manager," the state avoids altogether the problem the *Lucas* court addresses: whether a regulation (under the police power) of land so economically depresses the value of property so as to be a constitutionally protected taking for which compensation is due to the landowner.

This is not to suggest that all manner of coastal zone regulations now (or previously) acceptable under current notions of the police power can be simply readopted or reconstrued as public trust/property management rules.[11] Some no doubt can be, depending upon interpretations of the very sparse case law in Hawaii on the subject. Our courts have been expansive in setting out the scope of quasi-public trusts and the rights of beneficiaries, for example, in dealing with native Hawaiian rights and ceded lands.[12]

Private Land-Use Controls: Covenants, Servitudes, and Easements

Much developable land in Hawaii is held privately. The notion of view, resource protection, and conservation as marketing tools has not been lost on the land development community. The use of covenants and easements in land development documents is already a common practice. The preservation of view corridors in Waialae Iki and beach access and common areas in Black Point and Kahala has already provided a measure of amenity in these areas without resort to the police power. This is not to suggest, however, that such techniques are free of hassle. Neighborhood disputes over the setback of houses from streets in Kahala and the expansion of "remodeled" homes into neighbors' "view planes" toward the ocean in Waialae Iki demonstrate that such private controls must be privately enforced as well.

Such private agreements affecting land are enforceable in court by means of lawsuits between those who can show they are the beneficiaries of such agreements and those who are violating them.

Indeed, our state courts have required those who knowingly and willfully violate these agreements to remove the portions of their buildings in violation of them. Such limits as there are on private land-use controls—racially restrictive covenants are illegal and unenforceable, for example—are largely irrelevant to resource protection.

Thus, it is both legal and useful not only for private landowners to agree among themselves for such protections, but also for government as landowner as well. Any land or interest in land that the government transfers can be conditioned with covenants restricting its use as much or as little as government chooses to impose, without regard to the need for satisfying police power requirements or to concerns over regulatory takings. The state or a county could, for example, transfer land to a developer with heavy restrictions on density and use, together with massive open space and viewplane dedication requirements, and use the funds from the sale to compulsorily purchase other private land in danger of overdevelopment. The land sold could never be used without the restrictions imposed by the government as previous "owner," and the "condemned" land, now government-owned, would be entirely free of development or not, as the government as owner chooses. None of this invokes the state police power. The use and purchase must merely be for a public purpose, which courts have very broadly defined at least since the U.S. Supreme Court's decision in *Hawaii Housing Authority v. Midkiff* in 1985. Alternatively, the state could compulsorily acquire the development rights over key parcels of real estate in order to prevent unwanted development. Having paid for these rights, no issue of taking arises, regulatory or otherwise.

These are just a few of the ways that covenants and servitudes (including development and air rights) can be imaginatively used to accomplish the public welfare/preservation purposes now at considerable legal risk if done by regulation under the police power. Though the purchase of some or all of these rights will involve the expenditure of public funds, this very public cost will prevent the exercise of these techniques in all but the most critical preservation/conservation circumstances, while at the same time compensating the landowner for any loss of rights involved.

Due Process and Simplifying/Expediting Development Permissions

The State of Hawaii may be on the verge of finally shortening the process of land development approvals. The 1992 legislature passed a statute requiring both the counties and state agencies, by the end of 1993, to set relatively short limits on processing land-use permits and changes, and convene task forces and report progress to the legislature in the interim.

The counties have the longer period, probably in recognition that theirs is the more detailed look at land development projects, since in most instances the counties ultimately decide whether or not a landowner's plans are acceptable. Each county is required to enact ordinances by December 31, 1993, "to decrease, to not more than twelve months, the total time required by the county to review and, if appropriate, grant, all general plan, development plan, community plan, zone change and discretionary permit approvals to construct housing in that county." The time is reduced to six months for processing and approving subdivision, grading, building, and other ministerial development permits.

This is no small feat—nor a small savings to potential home buyers. The shorter time period from concept to construction will result in a lower cost to the land developer and, potentially, the home buyer. As one local developer noted, if the interest on a construction loan alone is $500,000 and he can save half of that, that's $1,000 per unit on a 250-unit residential development. Reducing a contractor's typical $70,000 per month overhead by simplifying regulations at that stage could save another $1,000 per month.[13] This is in addition to substantial savings in landholding costs. Moreover, if the processing time can be thus reduced for housing, why not for commercial and industrial developments as well?

In this context, state processing time for such as Land Use Commission boundary amendments from conservation, agricultural, and rural districts to urban are also important, as is other state agency action. The same new statute requires each state agency to "adopt such rules as may be necessary to decrease, to not more than six months, the total time required to review and, if appropriate, grant approvals to construct housing in this State."

These are welcome first steps in permit streamlining and simplification, which would do much to reduce the eight to ten years that some landowners have claimed it takes to obtain the necessary approvals for projects, including those that consist primarily of housing.

Biodiversity Protection by Agreement

Finally, there is the innovative California process of protecting biodiversity through public/private multiparty agreements. The brainchild of some of the country's most imaginative resource protection advocates and attractive to the administration of Governor Pete Wilson, the process contemplates bringing together all the federal, state, and local government agencies and affected landowners to set aside areas for the protection of plant and animal species in their natural landscape/habitat. As a first step, the State of California convened a meeting of nine federal and state land management agencies in 1991, all of which signed a memorandum of understanding on biological diversity in order to coordinate their conservation and preservation efforts. The purpose of the process is to identify geographical areas for species protection with the cooperation of private landholders and local governments, acting through an executive council.[14] Whether the memorandum will fulfill its promise of coordination and cooperation or become another layer of government remains to be seen, but it is a promising blend of regulatory coordination and agreement that may provide a mechanism worth emulating.

Summary

The State of Hawaii and its four counties must redefine their roles in the land conservation, preservation, and development process. The regulatory regime that has served government reasonably well for thirty years is extremely vulnerable both in terms of law and policy. Recent decisions by the U.S. Supreme Court make it crystal clear that business as usual, whether in connection with the built or the natural environment, can too easily be characterized as regulatory takings of property under the Fifth and Fourteenth Amendments of the U.S. Constitution. Moreover, the likelihood of lawsuits invoking these amendments in federal or state court is substantially increased as the "players" in the land-use game come increasingly from outside Hawaii. Mainland-based landowners with only a project or two in Hawaii and substantial resources outside the state are unlikely to be particularly concerned about alienating Hawaii officials by suing them for taking their property by regulation. Nor are such "outsiders" likely to be as culturally adverse to aggressively pursuing legal remedies through the courts. For all of these reasons, the regulatory system cannot continue to be the principal guardian of what we may want to preserve and conserve.

Instead, quasi-public bodies such as the Nature Conservancy and Historic Hawaii Foundation, alone or in conjunction with public-private ventures such as those proposed by PATH, are the probable wave of the future. Coupled with public "private-acting" agencies like HFDC, these bodies can pursue goals such as afford-able housing, historic and other built environment preservation, open space and coastal zone conservation and preservation, and environmental protection through agreement (development or oth-erwise) and cooperation, rather than the confrontation that has characterized regulatory enforcement through the police power. It is time to put aside the sword and shield of complaint and defense, wielded by landowner and government alike, and resolve differ-ences over land development and conservation priorities together. There is little that either government or landowner can do by themselves, but much they can accomplish together. It's about time they tried.

Notes

Chapter 1. Regulatory Takings

1. Fred P. Bosselman, David L. Callies and John S. Banta, *The Taking Issue*, (Washington: Council on Environmental Quality, 1973).

2. *Keystone Bituminous Coal Ass'n v. DeBenedictis*, 480 U.S. 470, 107 S. Ct. 1232 (1987), 94 L. Ed. 2d 472 (1987); *First English Evangelical Lutheran Church of Glendale v. County of Los Angeles*, 482 U.S. 304, 107 S. Ct. 2378 (1987), 96 L. Ed. 2d 250 (1987); *Nollan v. California Coastal Commission*, 483 U.S. 825, 107 S. Ct. 3141, 97 L. Ed. 2d 677 (1987).

3. *Keystone Bituminous Coal Association v. DeBenedictis.*

4. *First English Evangelical Lutheran Church of Glendale v. County of Los Angeles.*

5. *Nollan v. California Coastal Commission.*

6. *Lucas v. South Carolina Coastal Council*, 112 S. Ct. 2886, 505 U.S. _____, 120 L. Ed. 2d 798 (1992).

7. *PFZ Properties, Inc. v. Rodrigues*, _____ U.S. _____, 112 S. Ct. 2001, 118 L. Ed. 2d 597 (1992).

8. *Yee v. City of Escondido*, 503 U.S. _____, 112 S. Ct. 1522, 118 L. Ed. 2d 153 (1992).

Chapter 2. Preserving Open Space

1. *Hawaii Revised Statutes (HRS)*, chap. 205 (1985 Repl. and 1992 Supp.).

2. Callies, *Regulating Paradise: Land Use Controls in Hawaii*, 6–7, chap. 2, notes 4–7.

3. Callies, *Regulating Paradise*, 7; *State of Hawaii Data Book*, 176.

4. *HRS* § 205–2(d). Golf courses are permitted "provided they are not located within agricultural district lands with soil classified by the land study bureau's detailed land classification as overall (master) productivity rating class A or B."

5. Ibid., § 205–4.5.

6. State of Hawaii Land Evaluation and Site Assessment Commission, *A Report on the State of Hawaii Land Evaluation and Site Assessment System*, Legislative Reference Bureau, February 1986.

7. *HRS* § 205–5(b) and 205–6. Specially permitted uses under fifteen acres that are reasonable and unusual in nature may be permitted by the counties alone in both the agricultural and rural districts.

8. *Maha'ulepu v. Land Use Commission*, 71 Haw. 332, 790 P.2d 906 (1990). See Ushijima, Douglas K., "*Maha'ulepu v. Land Use Commission: A Symbol of Change*; Hawaii Land Use Law Allows Golf Course Development on Prime Agricultural Land by Special Use Permit," *U. Haw. L. Rev.* 13 205 (1991).

9. Office of State Planning (OSP), *Golf Course Development in Hawaii: Impacts or Policy Recommendations*, 3. An interesting question arises over just what county permissions are needed for golf courses on state-classified agricultural lands. It is clear, for example, that golf courses on prime agricultural land need county approval wherever located, since golf courses are permitted only as a special use on such lands. Arguably, county-administered shoreland management area permits (SMAs) are also necessary for the part of any golf course that is likely to be in the coastal zone, all as discussed in chapter 6. But what about golf courses on marginal agricultural land? HRS § 205–2(d) specifically lists golf courses among uses that (except for the above soils restriction) "shall" be permitted. How, then, could a county determine where in the state agricultural district golf courses may or may not locate? Surely the general language contained in 205–5 (a) that "Except as herein provided, the powers granted to counties under section 46–4 [the county zoning enabling act] shall govern the zoning within the districts, other than in the conservation districts" cannot take precedence over such a specific grant of rights to develop golf courses, "provided herein" elsewhere in the Land Use Law!

10. David Ramsour, "Harvesting a New Export Crop in Hawaii," (unpublished paper); Randall W. Roth, ed., *Paying For Paradise* (Honolulu: Mutual Publishing, 1992), chap. 25.

11. OSP, *Golf Course Development in Hawaii*, at 43.

12. State of Hawaii Land Evaluation and Site Assessment Commission, *A Report on the State of Hawaii Land Evaluation and Site Assessment System*.

13. OSP, *Golf Course Development in Hawaii*, table 6 and p. 66.

14. Ibid., 36–47.

15. Ibid., iii. Actually, this is the first of two recommendations in the report, the second of which, presuming there is no such new fifth open space district, would permit golf courses in agricultural districts only as a special use and only on the neighbor islands. As appears elsewhere in this book, this strikes me as an unduly restrictive attitude toward a particular use, the unpopularity of which has precious little to do with its land-use characteristics. For further and far more critical comment on the current bashing of golf course development, see Ramsour, note 10 above.

16. Senate Bill no. 1342 (1991 session).

17. Ibid., 9.

18. Ibid., 5.

19. Callies, *Regulating Paradise*, 7; Purcell, "Residential Use of Hawaii's Conservation Districts," *U. Haw. L. Rev.* 14 (1992): 187.

20. *HRS* § 183–41, as modified by recent amendments to HRS § 205–2.

21. Ibid., § 205–2(e).

22. See, e.g., Town and Yuen, "Public Access to Beaches in Hawaii: 'A Social Necessity'," *Haw. B.J.* 10 (Spring 1973): 3; David C. Slade, *Putting the Public Trust Doctrine to Work: The Application of the Public Trust Doctrine to the Management of Lands, Waters and Living Resources of the Coastal States.*

23. *HRS* § 183–41.

24. Ibid., § 183–41(c)(3).

25. *Hawaii Administrative Rules (HAR)*, § 13–2–1 to 14. See also Callies, *Regulating Paradise*, 9.

26. *HAR* § 13–2-15.

27. Upheld in *Stop H-3 Ass'n v. State Dept. of Transp.*, 706 P.2d 446 (Haw. 1985).

28. Hawaii Administrative Regulation 13–21(c). Conditions include compatibility with local and surrounding areas, appropriateness to physical conditions and land capability, harmonization with the environment, and preservation of natural beauty. See Purcell, note 19, above 198.

29. Eckbo, Dean, and Austin and Williams, *State of Hawaii Land Use Districts and Regulations Review*, (Honolulu: State of Hawaii Land Use Commission, 1969), 86.

30. Ibid., 87.

31. For a thorough discussion, see Purcell, note 19 above, 210 *et seq.*

32. For further discussion, see Purcell, note 19 above, 216 *et seq.*

33. For Honolulu, see Land Use Ordinance (LUO) § 5.10.

34. Act 100, *HRS* § 226–52.

35. *HRS* § 46–4(a).

36. Honolulu Revised Charter (HRC) § 5–409.

37. Ibid., § 5–412(3).

38. Residential, low-density apartment, medium-density apartment, high-density apartment, commercial, industrial, resort, agricultural, public and quasi-public, parks and recreation, preservation, and military.

39. These districts include: P-1 restricted preservation; F-1 military and federal preservation; P-2 general preservation; AG-1 restricted agricultural; AG-2 general agricultural; C country; R-20, R-10, R-7.5, R-5, R-3.5 residential; A-1 low-density apartment; A-2 medium-density apartment; A-3 high-density apartment; AMX-1 low-density apartment mixed use; AMX-2 medium-density apartment mixed use; AMX-3 high-density apartment mixed use; R resort; B-1 neighbor-

hood business; B-2 community business; BMX-3 community business mixed use; BMX-4 central business mixed use; I-1 limited industrial; I-2 intensive industrial; I-3 waterfront industrial; IMX-1 industrial-commercial mixed use; Hawaii Capital special district; Diamond Head special district; Punchbowl special district; Chinatown special district; Thomas Square/Honolulu Academy of Arts special district; Waikiki special district; Haleiwa special district. LUO arts. 2, 5, and 7.

40. *HRS* § 46–4(a)(1)–(12).

41. LUO § 5.10.

42. Ibid., § 5.10.

43. Ibid., § 5.10–1.

44. Ibid., Tables 3–A and 3–B.

45. 649 F. Supp. 926 (D. Hawaii 1986), affirmed 898 F.2d 112, opinion issued 899 F.2d 18, opinion amended and superceded 913 F.2d 573, *cert denied* 111 S.Ct. 1414.

46. *HRS* § 205–18. First conducted in 1969, the reviews ceased for the decade following the 1974 review when the statutory language so providing was deleted then later reintroduced into the Land Use Law.

47. OSP, *State Land Use District Boundary Review, Oahu* (1992); OSP, *State Land Use District Boundary Review, Hawaii* (1992); OSP, *State Land Use District Boundary Review, Maui, Molokai, Lanai* (1992).

48. E.g., OSP, *State Land Use District Boundary Review, Hawaii* (1992), 157.

49. *Pennsylvania Coal Co. v. Mahon*, 260 U.S. 393, 67 L. Ed. 322, 43 S. Ct. 158 (1922).

Chapter 3. Preserving the Built Environment

1. For a summary of the regulatory framework in Hawaii, see Ma'a, *Laws of Historic Preservation in Hawaii*; Callies, *Regulating Paradise*, chap. 6.

2. *HRS* § 6E–8(a).

3. Ibid., § 6E–2.

4. Ibid., § 6E–8(c).

5. Ibid., § 6E–5.5 (1980).

(b) The review board shall:

(1) Order and enter historic properties into the Hawaii register of historic places on the basis of their value to Hawaii's heritage;

(2) Evaluate and, when appropriate, recommend the nomination of historic properties to the national register of historic places[.]

Ibid., § (b). A historic property is defined as "any building, structure, object, district, area, or site, including heiau and underwater site, which is over fifty years old." *HRS* § 6E–2 (Supp. 1990). The board's criteria for registration and nomination are adopted pursuant to statutory direction.

6. Ibid., § 6E–10(a).

7. Ibid., § 343–5(a)(4).

8. Ibid., § 6E–15.

9. Ibid., § 43.

10. LUO §§ 7.30, 7.60, 7.70, and 7.90, respectively.

11. See, e.g., LUO §§ 7.90–4 pertaining to the Haleiwa district.

12. *HRS* §§ 205A-2(b)(2) and 205A–29.

13. LUO §§ 7.40, 7.50, 7.80, and 7.30, respectively.

14. Ibid., § 7.30–1.

15. Ibid., § 7.30–4.

16. See LUO § 7.20–5.

17. For analysis and examples of this national trend, see Costonis, *Icons and Aliens: Law, Aesthetics and Environmental Change.*

18. Ibid., 90–92.

19. 438 U.S. 104 (1978).

20. Such transfer by creating "zoning lots" so that adjacent "record" lot densities can be "loaded up" on one lot of record with the permission of the various record lot owners to produce one large building rather than several smaller ones has been common practice in New York for decades. See, e.g., Norman Marcus, "Air Rights Transfer in New York City," *Law and Contemporary Problems* 36 (1971): 372.

21. See, e.g., *The Society of Jesus of New England v. Boston Landmarks Commission*, 585 NE 2d 326 (1992). For a recent case upholding a church designation on the grounds the church failed to carry the burden of showing how the designation interfered with its religious practices (the church wanted to develop the site commercially), see *The Rector, Wardens, and Members of the Vestry of St. Bartholomew's Church v. the City of New York*, 914 F.2d 348 (2d Cir. 1990), *cert. denied*, 111 S.Ct. 1103 (1991).

22. *United Artists Theater Circuit, Inc. v. City of Philadelphia*, 595 A. 2d 6 (Pa. 1991).

23. *Agins v. Tiburon*, 447 U.S. 255; 100 S. Ct. 2138; 65 L. Ed. 2d 106 (1980), and the California Court of Appeals decision in *First English Evangelical Lutheran Church of Glendale v. County of Los Angeles*, 258 Cal. Rep. 893 (1989) on remand from the USSCT's decision of the same name, 482 U.S. 304; 107 S. Ct. 2378; 96 L. Ed. 2d 250 (1987).

24. For full discussion, see William Murtagh, *Keeping Time: The History and Theory of Preservation in America.*

Chapter 4. Exactions and Development Conditions

1. See, e.g., the county zoning enabling legislation at *HRS* §46–4.

2. *HRS* 46–142 *et seq.* (1992).

3. Callies, "Impact Fees, Exactions and Paying for Growth in Hawaii," *U. Haw. L. Rev.* 11 (1989): 295; Brian W. Blaesser and Christine M. Kentopp, "Impact Fees: The Second Generation," *Wash. U.J. Urb. & Contemp. L. Rev.* 28 (1990): 55; Julian Conrad Juergensmeyer, *Funding Infrastructure: Paying the Costs of Growth Through Impact Fees and Other Land Regulation Charges*, Lincoln Institute of Land Policy Monograph 85–5 (February 1985); David L. Callies and Robert H. Freilich, *Cases and Materials on Land Use*, (St. Paul, Minn.: West Publishing Co., 1986), chap. 4.

4. See, e.g., *Hernando County v. Budget Inns of Fla., Inc.*, 555 So.2d 1319 (Fla. Dist. Ct. App. 1990); *Frisella v. Town of Farmington*, 550 A.2d 102 (N.H. 1988); *Baltica Constr. Co. v. Planning Bd. of Franklin Tp.*, 537 A.2d 319 (N.J. App. 1987); *Batch v. Town of Chapel Hill*, 387 S.E.2d 655 (N.C. 1990); *Unlimited v. Kitsap County*, 750 P.2d 651 (Wash. App. 1988).

5. Ira Michael Heyman and Gilhool, "The Constitutionality of Imposing Increased Community Costs on New Suburban Residents Through Subdivision Exactions," *Yale L.J.* 73 (1964): 1119. See also Fred P. Bosselman and Nancy Stroud, "Legal Aspects of Development Exactions," in *Development Exactions*, ed. Frank and Rhodes (Chicago: Planners Press, 1987).

6. See Bosselman and Stroud, "Legal Aspects," 74.

7. Bosselman and Stroud, "Mandatory Tithes: The Legality of Land Development Linkage," *Nova L.J.* 9 (1985): 381, 397–99; see also *Holmdel Builders Ass'n v. Township of Holmdel*, 583 A.2d 277 (N.J. 1990).

8. 483 U.S. 825 (1987).

9. Ibid., 838–839. For full discussion, see David L. Callies and Malcolm Grant, "Paying for Growth and Planning Gain: An Anglo-American Comparison of Development Conditions, Impact Fees and Development Agreements," *Urban Lawyer* 23 (Spring 1991):221.

10. 483 U.S. 836–837. See also Bosselman and Stroud, "Mandatory Tithes"; Callies, "Impact Fees, Exactions and Paying for Growth in Hawaii"; Brenda Valla, "Linkage: The Next Stop In Developing Exactions," Growth Management Studies Newsletter 2 (4) (June 1987); Jerold S. Kayden and Robert Pollard, "Linkage Ordinances and Traditional Exactions Analysis," *Law & Contemporary Problems* 50 (Winter 1987): 127; Rachelle Alterman, "Evaluating Linkage and Beyond," *Wash. U.J. Urb. & Contemp. Law* (1988): 3; Callies and Freilich, Cases and Materials on Land Use. But see *Holmdel Builders Ass'n v. Township of Holmdel* (upholding impact fees for housing as functional equivalents of mandatory set-asides, which the court had already approved under New Jersey's constitutionally based "fair share" doctrine).

11. See *Home Builders and Contractors Ass'n of Palm Beach County v. Board of County Comm'rs of Palm Beach County Inc*, 469 U.S. 976; 105 S. Ct. 376; 83 L. Ed. 2d 311 (1984); *Hollywood, Inc. v. Broward County*, 431 So. 2d 606 (Fla.

App. 4 Dist. 1983); *Coulter v. City of Rawlins*, 662 P.2d 888 (Wyo. 1983); *Contractors and Builders Association of Pinellas County v. City of Dunedin*, 444 U.S. 867; 100 S. Ct. 140; 62 L. Ed. 2d 91 (1979).

12. See Callies and Grant, "Paying for Growth and Planning Gain," 231–239; James C. Nicholas, Arthur C. Nelson, and Julian C. Jeurgensmeyer, *A Practitioner's Guide to Development Impact Fees* (Chicago: Planners Press, 1991).

13. See, e.g., *Town of Longboat Key v. Lands End Ltd.*, 433 So.2d 574 (Fla. Dist. Ct. App. 1983); *Lafferty v. Payson City*, 642 P.2d 376 (Utah 1982); *Home Builders Ass'n of Central Arizona, Inc. v. Riddel*, 510 P.2d 376 (Ariz. 1973). See, generally, Juergensmeyer, *Funding Infrastructure*; Robert Mason Blake and Julian Conrad Juergensmeyer, "Impact Fees: An Answer to Local Governments' Capital Funding Dilemma," *Land Use & Envtl. L. Rev.* 14 (Annual 1987): 247.

14. To date at least nine states have passed impact fee enabling statutes: Arizona, California, Florida, Hawaii, Indiana, Maryland, Nevada, Texas, and West Virginia.

15. Callies and Grant, "Paying for Growth and Planning Gain," 228–229.

16. See, e.g., Illinois. See Wendy U. Larsen, "Impact Fees: Et tu Illinois," *J. Marshall L. Rev.* 21 (Spring 1988): 489.

17. *HRS* § 46–142 (1992) (enabling statute) and *HRS* § 46–148 (1992) (limiting impact fees to development driven "proportionate share"). For further comment on this new legislation, see James C. Nicholas and Dan Davidson, *Impact Fees in Hawaii: Implementing State Law* (Land Use Research Foundation of Hawaii 1992).

18. Nicholas, Nelson, and Juergensmeyer, *A Practitioner's Guide*, 9.

19. See, e.g., *HRS*, Chap. 64 (enabling statutes specific for Hawaii County); Hawaii Co. Code chap. 2, art. 7 (planning); chap. 17 (plumbing); chap. 15 (parks and recreation); chap. 26 (fire department). [Hawaii County Charter provisions.]

20. An exception is a road impact fee for West Maui, which, according to Maui officials, is virtually unused. Maui County code 14.62.080 (1988).

21. OSP, *Golf Course Development in Hawaii*.

22. See, e.g., David Waite, "Council OKs Royal Kunia Golf Deal," *Honolulu Advertiser*, February 14, 1991, A1; William Kresnak, "Fasi Says Fee Too Low, Vetoes Zoning," *Honolulu Advertiser*, March 1, 1991, A8; William Kresnak, "Fasi Defends Making Golf Course Developers Chip In," *Honolulu Advertiser*, September 7, 1991, A3.

23. See, e.g., David Waite, "Transit Plan Clears Hurdle," *Honolulu Advertiser*, May 2, 1991, A3 (describing council proposal for $25 million across-the-board golf course impact fee); Andy Yamaguchi, "Council's Bill on Golf Courses Falls Below Par," *Sunday Star-Bulletin & Advertiser*, October 13, 1991, A11.

24. *Commercial Builders of Northern Cal. v. City of Sacramento*, 112 S. Ct. 1997; 118 L. Ed. 2d 593 (1992).

25. Fees linking development generally to impacts on environmentally sensitive areas are newly passed in California, but so far untested in court. See Arthur Nelson and James C. Nicholas, and Lindell L. Marsh, "New-Fangled Impact Fees," *Planning*, American Planning Association, October 1992, pp. 20–24.

26. LUO 8.40.

27. Ibid., 8.40–C.

28. Ibid., 8.40–E.

29. See Callies and Freilich, *Cases and Materials on Land Use*, chap. 2. Development agreements authorized by statute are a way around the problem of bargaining away the police power, as discussed at the end of Chapter 4.

30. For cases criticizing this practice, see *Carlino v. Whitpain Investors*, 453 A.2d 1385 (Pa. 1982) and *Cederberg v. City of Rockford*, 291 N.E. 2d 249 (Ill. App. 1973).

31. See Hagman and Myscinski, *Windfalls for Wipeouts: Land Value Capture and Compensation*; Desmond Heap, *Introducing the Land Commission Act*, (London: Sweet and Maxwell, 1967).

32. These two laws are found, respectively in *HRS* chap. 226 and chap. 205.

33. *HRS* § 226–52(b)(2)(D).

34. Ibid., § 205–17(3).

35. Ibid., § 226–19(a).

36. Ibid., § 226–19(b).

37. Ibid., § 226–106.

38. Ibid., § 205–17(3)(F).

39. See *Commercial Builders of Northern Cal. v. City of Sacramento*, 112 S. Ct. 1997; 118 L. Ed. 2d 593 (1992).

40. See *Holmdel Builders Ass'n v. Township of Holmdel*; *So. Burlington Co. NAACP. v. Township of Mt. Laurel*, 336 A.2d 713 (N.J. 1975).

41. Callies and Grant, "Paying for Growth and Planning Gain."

42. OSP, *Golf Course Development in Hawaii*, 81.

43. See *Carlino v. Whitpain Investors*.

44. See note 14 above.

45. See, e.g., West's Ann. Cal. Gov. Code § 65864 *et. seq.* (California); *HRS* § 46–121 *et. seq.* (Hawaii).

46. *HRS* § 46–121 *et. seq.*; see Jan Sullivan, "Considerations in Implementing Hawaii's Development Agreements Statute," *Haw. Bar J.* 20 (1987): 87; Lyle Hosoda, "Development Agreements Legislation in Hawaii," *U. Haw. L. Rev.* 7 (1985): 173.

47. County of Hawaii Bill no. 593 (1993).

48. Richard Cowart, Kresmodel, and Stewart, *Development Agreements: Widespread Use Exceeds Expectations*, 1986 Quarterly Report, Center for Real Estate and Urban Economics, University of California, Berkeley (fourth quarter).

49. Deering s. 65865, West Supp. 1977 (Cal. Gov. Code Art. 2.5, chap. 4, title 7, amended in 1984).

50. While there is some recent commentary suggesting the need for a "nexus" between those items which a developer has agreed to contribute under a development agreement and the needs generated by that development, particularly after the *Nollan* case, these suggestions confuse the use of *regulatory* authority and the exercise of contract rights. See, for example, John Delaney, "Development Agreements: The Road From Prohibition to 'Let's Make a Deal,'" *The Urban Lawyer* 25 (1993): 49; Erin Johnson and Edward Zeigler, *Development Agreements*, Rocky Mountain Land Use Institute, Research Monograph no. 1 (1993), 19. See OSP, *Golf Course Development in Hawaii*.

51. HCDA, *Overview of Affordable Housing Targets*, December 1991, 4.

52. These and other figures in this discussion are taken from *Overview of Affordable Housing Targets* and a speech by HFDC's director, Joe Conant, delivered February 2, 1992, at a monthly meeting of the American Planning Association, Hawaii Chapter, in Honolulu.

53. OSP, *Golf Course Development In Hawaii*, 46.

Chapter 5. "Ordinary Delay"

1. *First English Evangelical Lutheran Church of Glendale v. County of Los Angeles*.

2. *PFZ Properties v. Rodrigues* (writ for certiorari dismissed as improvidently granted).

3. Section 1983 of the 1870 Civil Rights Act provides damage remedies for violation of individual civil rights under color of state law. The USSCT in *Monell v. Department of Social Services*, 436 U.S. 658 (1978) held that local governments are liable for such violations, and furthermore, that deprivation of property rights—through zoning, for example—is actionable under Section 1983, giving rise to hundreds of such claims throughout the United States. See Freilich and Carlisle, *Takings, Section 1983, and Land Use Disputes*, (Prentice Hall Law and Business, 1988). Freilich and Carlisle, sec. 1983 Sword and Shield, ABA Press, 1983.

4. See, e.g., Kelly, *Managing Community Growth*, 182–184; Coyle, *Property Rights and the Constitution*, chaps. 5 and 8. Bosselman, Feurer, and Siemon, *The Permit Explosion*.

5. Bosselman, Feurer, and Siemon, *The Permit Explosion*, 19–20.

6. Garrett Power, "Multiple Permits, Temporary Takings, and Just Compensation," *The Urban Lawyer* 23 (1991): 449, 457–458.

7. Andy Yamaguchi, "Home Builders Cite 7-Year Red Tape," *Sunday Star-Bulletin & Advertiser*, February 2, 1992, A7.

8. Ibid.

9. 482 U.S. 304 (1987).

10. 482 U.S. 321.

11. Fred P. Bosselman and David L. Callies, *The Quiet Revolution in Land Use Controls*, (Washington: Council on Environmental Quality, 1972), chap. 1; Callies, *Regulating Paradise*, chap. 1.

12. HRS §§ 205–2, 205–4.5, and 205–5(b) (1985 Repl. and 1991 Supp.).

13. Ibid., 205–6 (1985 Repl. and 1991 Supp.).

14. Indeed, the Hawaii Supreme Court has made it quite clear that such special permits are no substitute for the boundary amendment process if the proposed use is significantly out of character with the district in which the land is located—such as a sixty-acre theme park in the agricultural district. *Neighborhood Board v. State Land Use Commission*, 639 P.2d 1097 (Haw. 1982).

15. HRS § 205–4 (1985 Repl. and 1991 Supp.).

16. *Administrative Rules of the Department of Land and Natural Resources*, subchapter 3.

17. Minutes of the Meeting of the Board of Land and Natural Resources, March 13, 1987.

18. *First English Evangelical Lutheran Church of Glendale v. County of Los Angeles*, 321.

19. 42 United States Code, Annotated (USCA) § 4321 *et seq.* (1977 and 1992 Supp.). See Callies, *Regulating Paradise*, 121–123.

20. *Matsumoto v. Brinegar*, 568 F.2d 1289 (9th Cir. 1978).

21. HRS 343–5(a) (1985 Repl. and 1991 Supp.).

22. 33 USCA § 1251 *et seq.* (1977 and 1992 Supp.); sec. 404 corps wetland permits, 33 USCA § 1344; sec. 402 NPDES permits 33 USCA § 1342.

23. 33 USCA § 1344 (1977 and 1992 Supp.).

24. 33 Code of Federal Regulations (CFR) § 328.3(b) (1992).

25. 33 USCA 1344(a) (1977 and 1992 Supp.); 33 CFR 323.3 and 323.4 (1992).

26. 33 CFR 320.4(a) (1992).

27. 33 CFR 325.4 (1992).

28. 33 CFR 320.4(e) (1992).

29. 40 CFR 230.1(d) (1991).

30. Sec. 404, 33 USCA § 1344(c) (1977 and 1992 Supp.).

31. 33 USCA § 1342 *et seq.* (1977 and 1992 Supp.).

32. HAR 11–55–1 *et seq.*

33. For discussion of these land-use regimes in Hawaii, see Callies, *Regulating Paradise*, chaps. 3, 4, 7, and 8.

34. See Bosselman and Callies, *The Quiet Revolution*; Richard F. Babcock and Clifford L. Weaver, *City Zoning: The Once and Future Frontier*, (Washington: Planners Press, 1979).

35. Land Use Ordinance of the City and County of Honolulu §§ 2.10, 2.20, and 2.30 (1991).

36. Callies, *Regulating Paradise*, chap. 2; Charles Goodin, "The Honolulu Development Plans," *U. Haw. L. Rev.* 6 (1984): 33; Kent M. Keith, "The Hawaii State Plan Revisited," *U. Haw. L. Rev.* 7 (Spring 1985): 29; see also *Lum Yip Kee v. Honolulu*, 767 P.2d 815 (Haw. 1989) and commentary thereon in David L. Callies, Mahilani E. Kellett, and Donna H. Kalama, "The Lum Court, Land Use and the Environment," *U. Haw. L. Rev.* 14 (1992): 119.

37. RCH 5–409.

38. Ibid., 5–407 to 5–412.

39. Ibid., 5–412(3).

40. Ibid., 5–411 to 5–413.

41. Ibid., 5–408 (1992 amendments).

42. Telephone conference with DGP director Robin Foster, April 1993, and Development Plans Briefing Booklet, DGP, April 1993.

43. RCH Art. VI, chaps. 9 and 10; LUO § 8.30.

44. LUO § 8.30.

45. Ibid., §§ 7.20, 8.30, and 8.30–8.

46. Callies, *Regulating Paradise*, 38.

47. RCH 6–909.

48. Ibid., 4–202; RCH 6–910 (1993).

49. Ibid., 6–909(b). The LUO simply refers to the charter for authority and standards in granting variances. See LUO § 1.50.

50. Callies, *Regulating Paradise*, 89–90.

51. *Topliss v. Plan. Comm. of Hawaii*, 842 P.2d 648 (Haw. App. 1993); *Mowry v. Kauai Plan. Comm'n*, _____ Haw. _____ (1993).

52. *Sandy Beach Defense Fund v. City Council*, 70 Haw. 361 (1989), discussed in Callies, Kalama, and Kellett, "The Lum Court, Land Use, and the Environment."

53. Rev. Ord. Honolulu 33–5.

54. Ibid., 84–4.

Chapter 6. Regulating for Environmental Protection

1. Callies, *Regulating Paradise*, chaps. 7–10.

2. 480 U.S. 470 (1987).

3. *California Coastal Commission v. Granite Rock Co.*, 480 U.S. 572; 107 S. Ct. 1419; 94 L. Ed. 2d 577 (1987).

4. For the views that police power can be used for welfare—as in protection of the environment, see Holly Doremus, "Patching the Ark: Improving Legal Protection of Biological Diversity," *Ecology L. Q.* 18 (1991): 265; Alison Rieser, "Eco-

logical Preservation as a Public Property Right: An Emerging Doctrine in Search of a Theory," *Harv. Env. L. Rev.* 15 (1991): 393; Carole Rose, "The Comedy of the Commons: Custom, Commerce and Inherently Public Property," *U. Chi. L. Rev.* 33 (1986): 711; Richard O. Brooks, "A New Agenda for Modern Environmental Law," *J. Env. L. & Litig.* 6 (1991): 1.

5. *Lucas v. South Carolina Coastal Council*, transcript of Supreme Court argument March 2, 1992.

6. Callies, *Regulating Paradise*, 87.

7. Ibid., 88.

8. *Topliss v. Plan. Comm. of Hawaii; Mowry v. Kauai Plan. Comm'n.*

9. *HRS* 205A–4(a) (1985 Repl. and 1991 Supp.).

10. Ibid., 205A–22 (1985 Repl. and 1991 Supp.).

11. Ibid., 205A–26 (1986 Repl. and 1991 Supp.).

12. Ibid.

13. 33 USCA 1344(a) (1977 and 1992 Supp.).

14. Blumm, "The Clean Water Act's Section 404 Permit Program Enters Its Adolescence: An Institutional and Programmatic Prospective," *Ecology L. Q.* 8 (1980):409.

15. 33 CFR. 320.4(a) (1992).

16. 33 CFR. 320.4(b)(2)(i)–(viii) (1992).

17. 33 CFR 320.4(e) (1992).

18. *Hoffman Estates v. EPA*, 902 F.2d 567 (7th Cir. 1990).

19. Callies, *Regulating Paradise*, chap. 8.

20. LUO 7.10–5.

21. Ibid., 7.10–7.

22. Professor Richard Epstein of the University of Chicago is said to espouse the extreme view that any government action that deprives a citizen of property without compensation is a constitutionally protected taking. *The Economist*, February 29, 1992, 28.

23. Callies, *Regulating Paradise*, chap. 10.

24. Hawaii Administrative Rules Title II Department of Health Chapter 60, Air Pollution Control Subchapter 3, Stationary Sources.

25. Ibid.

26. Jarman, "Hawaii," in Gerrard, ed., *Environmental Law Practice Guide*.

27. Callies, *Regulating Paradise*, chap. 11; Jarman, "Hawaii."

28. Ibid.

29. Title II, Department of Health, Chapter 55 Water Pollution Control, sec. 11–55–02.

30. Ibid., 11–55–04.

31. Hawaii Administrative Rules Title II Department of Health Chapter 54 Water Quality Standards, at 11–54–03(b)(2).

Chapter 7. Conclusion

1. See, e.g., Costonis, *Space Adrift: Saving Urban Landmarks Through the Chicago Plan*; Marcus, "Air Rights In New York City: TDR, Zoning Lot Merger and the Well-Considered Plan," *Brooklyn L. R.* 50 (1984):867.

2. *Penn Central Transportation Company v. New York*, 438 U.S. 104 (1978).

3. See LUO, § 4.40–21, Joint Development of Two or More Adjacent Zoning Lots. This technique was used recently in the construction of the Pan Pacific building on Bishop Street, where air rights on the adjoining Ritz building were transferred to the building site for Pan Pacific Plaza.

4. Madelyn Glickfeld, "New Strategies and Roles: Making Better Use of Governmental Acquisition Resources to Protect Environmentally Important Lands," presented at a UCLA Public Policy Conference, December 3, 1992, Los Angeles, California.

5. Joe Conant, American Planning Association speech, February 26, 1992.

6. See, e.g., *In Re Sanborn*, 57 Haw. 585 (1977) and *County of Hawaii v. Sotomura*, 55 Haw. 176 (1973).

7. See, e.g., *Just v. Marinette County*, 201 N.W. 2d 761 (Wisc. 1972); *National Audubon Society v. Superior Ct. of Alpine County*, 658 P.2d 709 (Cal. 1983); *Orion v. State*, 747 P.2d 1062 (Wash. 1987); *Kootenai Environment Alliance v. Panhandle Yacht Club*, 671 P.2d 1085 (Idaho 1983).

8. *State v. Kobayashi v. Zimring* 58 Haw. 106 (1977).

9. See cases collected and analyzed in Note, "Private Property Rights Yield to the Environmental Crisis: Perspectives on the Public Trust Doctrine" *S.C. L. Rev.* 41 (1990): 897; Note, "Lyon and Fogerty: Unprecedented Extension of the Public Trust," *Calif. L. Rev.* 70 (1982): 1138.

10. See, e.g., David C. Slade, *Putting the Public Trust Doctrine to Work: The Application of the Public Trust Doctrine to the Management of Lands, Waters and Living Resources of the Coastal States* (1990); "The Public Trust Doctrine and Coastal Management in Washington State," Wash. L. Rev. 67 (1992): 521.

11. E.g., *Bell v. Town of Wells*, 557 A.2d 168 (Maine 1988).

12. E.g., *Pele Defense Fund v. Paty*, 73 Haw. 578 (September 1992); *Public Access Shoreline Hawaii v. Hawaii Planning Commission* No. 15460 ICA Haw. App. (1993). 1993 Haw. App. Lexis 2.

13. James K. Schuler, as reported in Jerry Tune, "How Can Builders Slash Cost of Affordables?" *Sunday Star-Bulletin & Advertiser*, June 28, 1992, G1.

14. Michael Mantell, Undersecretary for Resources, State of California, "California's Biodiversity Strategy," prepared for a UCLA Public Policy Forum, Los Angeles, California, December 2, 1992.

References

Alterman, Rachelle, ed. *Private Supply of Public Services: Evaluation of Real Estate Exactions, Linkage, and Alternative Land Policies.* New York: New York University Press, 1988.

Blaesser, Brian W., and Alan C. Weinstein, eds. *Land Use and the Constitution.* Chicago: Planners Press, 1989.

Callies, David L. *Regulating Paradise: Land Use Controls in Hawaii.* Honolulu: University of Hawaii Press, 1984.

————., ed. *After Lucas: Land Use Regulation and the Taking of Property Without Compensation.* Chicago: ABA Press, 1993.

Costonis, John J. *Icons & Aliens: Law, Aesthetics and Environmental Change.* Urbana: University of Illinois Press, 1989.

Coyle, Dennis J. *Property Rights and the Constitution: Shaping Society through Land Use Regulation.* Albany, NY: State University of New York Press, 1993.

Cullingworth, J. Barry. *The Political Culture of Planning.* New York: Routledge, 1993.

Davidson, Dan, and Ann Usagawa. *Paying for Growth in Hawaii.* Honolulu: Land Use Research Foundation of Hawaii, 1988.

Frank, James E., and Robert M. Rhodes, eds. *Development Exactions.* Chicago: Planners Press, 1987.

Hill, G. Richard, ed. *Regulatory Taking: The Limits of Land Use Control.* 2d ed. Chicago: ABA Press, 1993.

Jarman, Casey M. "Hawaii." In *Environmental Law Practice Guide,* edited by Michael B. Gerrard. Albany, NY: Matthew Bender, 1992.

Johnson, Erin J., and Edward H. Ziegler. *Development Agreements: Research Monograph Series No. 1.* Denver: Rocky Mountain Land Use Institute, 1993.

Kelly, Eric Damien. *Managing Community Growth: Policies, Techniques and Impacts.* Westport, CT: Greenwood Publishing Group, Inc., 1993.

Korngold, Gerald. *Private Land Use Arrangements.* Colorado Springs: Shepards-McGraw, 1990.

Ma'a, Thalia Lani. *Laws of Historic Preservation in Hawaii*. Honolulu: Office of Hawaiian Affairs, 1988.

Malone, Linda A. *Environmental Regulation of Land Use*. Chicago: Clark Boardman Callaghan, 1990.

Murtagh, William J. *Keeping Time*. Pittstown, NJ: Main Street Press, 1989.

Myers, Phyllis. *Lessons from the States: Strengthening Land Conservation Programs through Grants to Nonprofit Land Trusts*. Washington, D.C.: Land Trust Alliance, 1992.

Nicholas, James C., Arthur C. Nelson, and Julian C. Juergensmeyer. *A Practitioner's Guide to Development Impact Fees*. Chicago: Planners Press, 1991.

Nicholas, James C., and Dan Davidson. *Impact Fees in Hawaii: Implementing the State Law*. Honolulu: Land Use Research Foundation of Hawaii, 1992.

Platt, Rutherford H. *Land Use Control: Geography, Law and Public Policy*. Englewood Cliffs, NJ: Prentice Hall, 1991.

Porter, Douglas R., and Lindell L. Marsh, eds. *Development Agreements, Practice Policy and Prospects*. Washington, D.C.: Urban Land Institute, 1989.

Rogers, William H. *Environmental Law*. 4 vols. St. Paul, MN: West Publishing Co., 1992.

Roth, Randall W, ed. *Paying For Paradise: Lucky We Live Hawaii?* Honolulu: Mutual Publishing, 1992.

Slade, David C. *Putting the Public Trust Doctrine to Work: The Application of the Public Trust Doctrine to the Management of Lands, Waters and Living Resources of the Coastal States*. Privately printed, 1990.

Smith, Zachary A., and Richard C. Pratt, eds. *Politics and Public Policy in Hawaii*. Albany, NY: State University of New York Press, 1992.

State of Hawaii. Office of State Planning. *Golf Course Development in Hawaii: Impacts or Policy Recommendations*. 1992.

Stone, Charles P., and Danielle B. Stone, eds. *Conservation Biology in Hawaii*. Honolulu: University of Hawaii Cooperative National Park Resource Studies Unit, 1989.

Wakeford, Richard. *American Development Control*. London: Her Majesty's Printing Office, 1990.

Want, William L. *Law of Wetlands Regulation*. Chicago: Clark Boardman Callaghan, 1989.

Index

Agricultural district (state): described, 12; uses permitted on, 12–17
Architectural controls: in Land Use Ordinance of Honolulu, 32

Biodiversity agreements: use in California to protect endangered species, 105
Boundary review: by Land Use Commission, 60

Charter, Honolulu: development plan requirements, 71; rezoning requirements, 73; variance procedure, 74
Clean Air Act: and State Health Department, 90; and State Implementation Plans (SIPs), 90; and stationary source standards, 90, 91; summarized, 90
Clean Water Act: and effluent standards, 93; and 404 Permits procedure, 64–65, 66; and National Pollution Discharge Elimination System (NPDES), 92, 93; and nonpoint sources of pollution, 92; NPDES permits, 66; and publicly owned wastewater treatment works (POTWs), 91; summarized, 91–92; and wetlands regulation, 64
Compensation: for property taken, 4
Conditional use permits: and the State Conservation District, 61

Conditional uses: and role of DLU director, 73-74; standards and procedures of (Honolulu LUO), 73–74
Conditional zoning, 46; and housing, 49; and unilateral agreements, 46
Conservation district: analyzed, 18, 19, 20; and CDUA application, 19; and CDUA permits for development, 61; and Lanikai Ridge decision, 21; and Mount Olomana decision, 20–21; nonconformities in, 19
Conservation district (state): and relationship to Honolulu LUO, 24–25; and subzones, 19; summarized, 17–18
Corps of Engineers 404 dredge and fill permits: EPA veto, 66; in hypothetical case, 2; procedure of, 64, 65; process of, 86; and public interest (aesthetics and historic properties) review, 65; and public interest review process and guidelines, 86, 87, 88
Covenants and servitudes, 102, 103

Department of General Planning (Honolulu): development plan duties, 72
Department of Health: and Clean Air Act, 90
Department of Land and Natural Resources: and historic preservation powers, 30; and state plan, 49

123

About the Author

David L. Callies is a professor in The William S. Richardson School of Law at the University of Hawaii. His areas of specialization are land use, real property, and local government law. He holds degrees from DePauw University, the University of Michigan, and Nottingham University in England. He is the author of *Regulating Paradise: Land Use Controls in Hawaii;* coauthor with Fred P. Bosselman and John S. Banta of *The Taking Issue*, with Robert H. Freilich of *Cases and Materials on Land Use*, and with Fred Bosselman of *The Quiet Revolution in Land Use Control;* and editor of *After* Lucas: *Land Use Regulation and the Taking of Property without Compensation.* He has written more than fifty articles on land-use policy.

Professor Callies has lectured on land-use policy in Japan, China, Hong Kong, American Samoa, Commonwealth of the Northern Marianas Islands, New Zealand, England, and Switzerland, and often serves as a legal advisor to the State of Hawaii and its counties.